MISS SLIMMENS' WINDOW,

AND OTHER PAPERS.

MISS ALVIRA SLIMMENS,

MILLINER

MISS SLIMMENS' WINDOW,

AND OTHER PAPERS.

BY MRS. MARK PEABODY.

With Humorous Illustrations from Designs by J. H. Howard.

NEW YORK:
DERBY & JACKSON, 119 NASSAU STREET,
1859.

Entered according to Act of Congress, in the year 1859, by
DERBY & JACKSON,
In the Clerk's Office of the District Court of the United States for the Southern
District of New York.

W. H. Tinson, Stereotyper.

Geo. Russell & Co., Printers.

CONTENTS.

MISS SLIMMENS'S WINDOW.

WHEN Miss Slimmens first hung out her sign as Fashionable Milliner, it was adorned with a bonnet after the following pattern:

The patterns inside of the shop-window have changed very frequently since then; but the sign remains as it was, except that its pristine glory is nearly obliterated by the wear and tear of the weather. But, if the bright yellow of the bonnet is faded, and its sky-blue bows are scarcely discernible, so have the roses faded that once bloomed on the cheeks of Miss Slimmens; and she has been compelled, for the last ten years at least, to resort to "artificials." She bleaches and trims to perfection—herself, as well as her bonnets; despite which, some of her neighbors have been heard to insinuate that the smell of brimstone about her premises did not proceed entirely from the covered barrel which sets in the back yard, and in which there are usually two or three wrecks of Leghorn hanging, as slimp and melancholy as the prospects of Miss Slimmens herself.

CHAPTER I.

YOU CAN'T CATCH OLD BIRDS WITH CHAFF.

THERE'S Stebbins's house been shut up three days, and not a sign of life about it. I wonder where he's sent the children to? I suppose to their grandmother's. Poor little things! it's cruel to think of their being orphans, and no telling what kind of a stepmother they'll get to knock 'em and beat 'em around, and schinch 'em in clothes and vittals. However, maybe their prospects is not so bad as they might be; *perhaps* they're soon agoing to have somebody to look after 'em who never had the name of taking the advantage of anybody, let alone stepchildren. Do you know why Stebbins had his house painted straw color, instid of white, and that sweet little portcullis put over the front door?

If you don't, somebody does. It was only the day before he had the men to work, he says to me, "Alvira"—Stebbins has called me by my given name ever since his wife died—"supposing *you* was going to have a house painted, what color would you prefer?" "La, now!" said I, "people's tastes differ; and, since the house *isn't* mine, and nobody has ever said it was going to be mine, what do you care what color I like best?" "Well," said he, "I knew you was considered the tastiest person in the village, used to all sorts of pretty colors in ribbons and trimmin's, and, as I don't purfess to have much knowledge of such things myself, I thought I'd ask you." Wasn't that a delicate way, now, of managing the matter, and letting the person most interested know that he'd like her opinion? I declare, my respect for Stebbins riz considerably! though I'd always thought well of him as a good man to his family, and a stiddy, industrious person, not bad-looking, either, though *rather* old for a girl in her twenties. Let's see? he must be full forty year old; and that would be fourteen years difference. So then I told him I was sick of these everlasting white houses, and that *I* thought peach-bloom or straw-color would look sweetly, and he thanked me, and asked if I could suggest any other improvement; and I fairly blushed at having him putting such questions to me, and I said: "Oh, Mr. Stebbins, if you'd really like my ideas on the subject, I think a handsome portcullis over the front door would make your house almost equal to Squire Higgins's." "The very thing!" said he; "and, if it don't cost too much, I shall have one right away."

What's that you say, Clara Brown? "Stebbins is apt to look at the cost of a thing before he gets it." Supposing he is, then; so is any prudent man; they'd be a fool not to. I guess there's some as have to work in this shop for seventy-five cents a week and their board would be glad of a chance to help spend what he's been so prudential as to lay up. Mind that shir you're running. You're getting it as crooked as one of Tim Button's stories; and that bunnit is for Mrs. Martingall, the particularest of all my customers.

What has Stebbins gone out of town for? I haven't insinuated that I knew, have I? He *may* be gone to Boston to get a new set of hair-bottomed chairs and a carpet for the front room before a certain ceremony comes off; but that's not saying that he *has*, nor that I know anything about his business. I *may* be going to make a wedding-bunnit for somebody not far away from this chair, out of this piece of white satin; but that's not saying that I am going to. Look here, Dora Adams, if you don't quit that everlasting giggling and snorting out a laughing, you'll quit my shop. How much work do you suppose you get done in a day, between looking at them red danglers that you set up half the night to put in papers, and snickering at goodness knows what every five minutes? "Your hair isn't red; it's orborn and curls naturally?" Humph! perhaps you'll get some fine young man to believe that, but not immejetly.

Just see that little, stuck-up Laura Griggs trotting along to school in her all-wool de laine dress, plenty good enough for Sundays. Her mother just does it to spite better people; but, if what report says is true, she'll soon be in the fix of the man that bit off his nose to spite his face. It's no matter what I mean. I'm never the first to spread bad news; and I don't intend to be now. People that live beyond their means must expect to be brought up with a short turn some time. When folks gets to sending to Boston and Lowell for their bunnits, because there's nothing in their own village good enough for 'em, it's time——

Wonder whose dog that *can* be? Girls, run here, and look, before he gets past the corner; that one with the crimpy tale, black and white. Did either of you ever see it before? "No?" Well, neither did I; and now somebody's got company, or somebody's been buying him. It's curious his master wasn't with him; being a strange dog, so, he'd be apt to have somebody with him to keep watch of him. He couldn't be a stray dog; he run along too contented for that. He's a beautiful fellow; such long, silky hair, such intelligent eyes, and such a curly—gracious! here he comes! not the dog, but his master! Yes, that must be him, for he's a stranger, and now he's whistling to him; and he's got on one of them new-fangled overcoats, and is *so* stylish! Dear me! I wish I knew who he was visiting, and what brought him to Pennyville, and how long he was going to stay. Goodness! he looked right straight in the window; and he must have seen *something* to admire, for he kept on looking full a minute. Girls, what are you peaking over my shoulder for? Get back to your work, you lazy, giggling things! I declare, I shall go crazy long before I'm thirty years old, if I have to keep track of two such idle snips! He's gone round the corner, now, toward Squire Higgins's. If Sabina Higgins caught *that* fish when she was away to her uncle's, she did more than I gave her credit for. Hand me that Leghorn flat. It's to be called for at sundown, and I've not made the first bow yet, nor put in the lining. If there wasn't so much gab going on in this shop, there'd be more work. I don't see what they wanted the flat so particularly to-night for. There's no picnic nor nothing going off that I've heard of, and it's three days to Sunday. Maybe Celestia's going to town with her father when he takes his grain to market. It's always hurry! hurry! hurry! Everybody hurries the milliner, just for the fun of it, I believe. There's one thing, Alvira Slimmens don't intend to be their slave much longer. She sighs for the repose of a straw-colored house, with a white portcullis to shade it, like the satin cape of a Leghorn bunnit. What's that? "getting poetical?" Supposing I am? Young people mostly are occasionally; and I don't see what's to prevent. There are but few in the interesting situation of an engagement but feels inclined, at times, to express their feelings in verse. There was some lines by somebody to somebody in the last number of the

"Pennyville Eagle," signed "J. S.;" and, if "J. S." don't stand for Joshua Stebbins, what does it stand for? I've answered them already, and shall send the verses over to the printer's to-night; but I wouldn't have anybody know for the world that I was an authoress. I wouldn't read 'em to anybody if I was asked; but I'll recite the last verse, because I know you'd like to hear it:

"Long as there's water in the sea,
Or planets in the heavens,
My heart shall only beat for thee,
My voice shall murmur ********"

I've left the last word stars, so that the public might not perceive too much of what is too sacred to betray. That blue ribbon, Clara! Blue is a sweet color. The language of blue is constancy. It's so romantic to have the virgin affections true to one——

For the land's sake! as true as I'm alive, if there isn't Stebbins come home—in a buggy, too—and a woman with him that ain't his mother! She's got white ribbin on her bunnit and a white veil; and he's helping her out as if he was treading on eggs. "She looks like a bride," hey?

was that what you said? She does, that's a fact; and I'll bet that heartless Stebbins has been up and getting married, without letting anybody know it, and his first wife scarcely cold in her grave. It's just ten months Tuesday since the funeral, when he took on so hard, the old hypocrite! I declare it makes me faint and sick to think of it; but I'm sure I need not be surprised, for he asked me long ago to take her place, but I refused him, with the uttermost indignation. I told him he ought to be ashamed of himself, and he a widower such a brief length o' time. Joshua Stebbins must a took me for a bigger fool than I am, to expect I was going to take up with a crooked stick at last, and two freckle-faced, quarrelsome, hateful little brats besides. I guess his new wife didn't know what she was coming home to; them children is the pest of the neighborhood. Humph! he helps her up the steps under that portcullis mighty pleasant now, and I suppose she's admiring things; but if she don't wait many a month before the stingy cretur gets anything more, and if she doesn't have to wear faded finery after a while, then I lose my guess. "You thought I approved Mr. Stebbins's prudence?" So I do approve of a proper degree of prudence in anybody; but nobody ever heard me say I upheld the right-up-and-down meanness of that man—his stinginess. Why, he'd steal the cents off a dead man's eyes, for all I knew! and I don't wish you to say again that I approve of him.

She's minced into the house, now, and he's tied his horse and gone in with her. I hope you'll be able to keep your eyes on your work, now there's no more to be seen. It seems as if my window was made for nothing in the world but for my apprentices to gap out at everything and everybody. There never was a woman tormented with two such idle minxes as you girls. Clara Brown, you're doing that all wrong! No, I didn't tell you to do it that way, neither. What do you mean by contradicting me? You will finish that job, now, before you go to bed, if it takes you till three o'clock in the mornin'; I won't pay girls for whispering, and talking, and looking out the window; I don't do it myself, and I don't allow it in others. I can just tell you what it is, I shan't try to get this flat trimmed for that high-flyer of a young miss; if she's disappointed, it's good enough for her. My head aches, and I ain't a-going to take another stitch to-day. Dora!—do you hear me?—go and put over the kettle; I want a good, strong cup o' tea. Don't bother me with questions; I ain't going to speak again this evening. I'm tired of your gabble, and I want silence for once in my life; and now, because you can't talk, talk, talk, I suppose you're wondering and wondering who the bride is, and what her name was, and how she looks, and where she come from, and how old she is, and what they're a-getting for supper, and whether you'll have a piece of the wedding-cake, and how he happened to get acquainted with her; but I'd jest advise you to mind your own business, and let other people's alone. I won't have it; so just quit it. You needn't be setting that tea to steeping just yet. I'm going to throw on my bunnit, and run over and call. I want to be the first to congratulate 'em, just to show Joshua Stebbins that I don't care a pin for him; though if somebody was a mind to sew him for a brich of promise, she might kick up a pretty muss in Pennyville; but you can't catch old birds with chaff, nor Alvira Slimmens with a widower.

CHAPTER II.

MISS SLIMMENS HAS HOPES.

ISN'T that old Dr. Greene—yes, it is—coming out of Peters's? Of course, Sarah Peters's got another baby! She and Queen Victory have run about an equal match, though I believe she's beat the queen by this last one; yes, this is her ninth. Well, I never thought she'd come to that when she and I used to be girls together—that is, she was a great big, and I was a very little, girl. It used to make her as mad as fire when she had to tend any of her own little sisters and brothers; she often said she hated young ones, and I hope she's got enough of 'em now. That comes of her not following my example, and jest saying "No!" right out, every time a simpleton of a male cretur, in pantaloons, come a-sugaring around and wanting to send for the minister. The pertinasty of some men is surprisin'! If I hadn't fit and fit against it, I might have been seduced into matrimony myself, and been in the same fix she is this blessed minit. Good Lord! I ought to be thankful for my delivery; it's bad enough bleaching, and trimming, and making up bunnits for a living, but it's not quite so bad as nine squalling, eating, teasing, worrying plagues to cook and mend for. The more I think on it, the more I thank my stars that I gave Stebbins the mitten as flat as I did.

Yes, it's another baby, sure enough; do hear the little panther yell! I wish they'd keep their windows shut, distracting decent people with their hullabaloo. If there's anything on airth I hate and despise, it's a little squirming, kicking, piny-faced, screeching baby. If I had that little red thing over here, I'd use it for a pincushion. What's that, Clara Brown? "You love the innocent things, and hope you'll get married some of these days, and have one of your own?" Ugh! I've a notion to turn you out of my shop, you indelicate, immodest young woman, you! What is the females of the present day coming to, when a chit of seventeen can confess that she ever even *thought* of such a thing? If I ever *should* be so overcome by persuasion as to consent to share the home of some being of the opposite sex, I trust that our affections will be of too spirituous a character to fulminate in a cradle and a bundle of squalling red flannel. Hey? I heard that whisper, Dora Adams. You said—and you needn't deny it—that if I waited much longer, you guessed there wouldn't be any danger. What did you mean by that? say! what did you mean? If you think your red curls and your sassy ways is going to excuse impudence to them that employs you, you're mistaken; and you've got to tell what you meant by that speech. "You meant that my beaux would become discouraged, and be obleeged to court somebody else?" Oh, that's not so bad as it might have been if you'd been saying what doesn't become you. I suppose *you're* looking for'ard to a chance, and maybe you'll get one when you grow out of looking so dowdy and fat. Your cheeks are like two poppies, and your waist is almost as big again as it ought to be; if I were in your place, I'd drink vinegar. There! you needn't roll them great eyes of yours over to Clara, as much as to say there is plenty of vinegar about. What did Celestia say because she didn't get her leghorn last night? "Almost cried," hey, and you "felt so sorry for her that you went to work and finished it?" Another one of your liberties, when you knew that I left it *on purpose* to disappoint her. It makes these chits altogether too selfish and conceited to have all their whims humored; a little vexation of spirit is good for 'em, once in a while.

How did I like Stebbins's new wife? I've no doubt he's done as well as an old widower with two young ones could expect to. I shouldn't think she was over thirty, and some folks might think she was good-looking, but her eyes is too black and sparkly, and her nose is pug, and she's too plump to have a particle of style about her. She's dreadful blushing and smiling now, but if them children don't see hard times before a year's gone by, then Alvira Slimmens isn't good at guessing. Stebbins looked as if he'd like to crawl through an auger-hole when he seen it was me, and he colored up like a beet when he introduced Mrs. Stebbins. I expect he saw I was eyeing her mighty sharp, for he kept hitching about, as uneasy as a fish out of water; but I catched them smiling in their sleeves when they thought I didn't take notice. I guess she was some poor body, that couldn't do any better, for her bunnit was as much as three months behind the fashion, and her silk gown was a kind of a slimsy thing. Did I leave that poetry I was speaking of at the printing-office, on my way home? Mercy sake alive! you're ruining that piece of satin, you careless thing! Lay it down, and go and bring me them satins, and hand me that ruche, and pick up them scraps off the carpet.

"La! Miss Peters's got another baby. As soon's I got my work done, I must drop in and see how she's getting along. The poor creture can't have much life left in her; and as for him, I don't see how he contrives to find bread and butter for so many mouths. I've a good notion to take her over some of my quince-jelly and one of them young chickens. No I won't, neither; I'm so provoked at her for being such a fool! She'll expect me to hold the young one, and kiss it, and make a fuss over it, when I'd rather choke the little rat. If ever there was a torment sent upon earth, it's children. They're worse than the seven plagues of Egypt—no peace, no quiet, no order where they are—greasing you up, and falling down and bumping themselves, scratching each other, littering up the floor, taking the measles, and the chickenpox, and the scarlet fever, wearing out their clothes, telling tales, stealing your sugar and preserves, crying with the stomach-ache, taking fits in the night, falling in the creek and getting drowned, they make a perfect panorama; and I only wonder their mothers don't go crazy with insanity. When there's any prospects of *my* having any, the Lord deliver me! Miss Peters's got Mother Lummis to nuss her; I see her pass through the hall just now. There's one of the children out in the street; I'll just call her over, and find out whether it's a girl or a boy. So! you've got a little sister, have you? oh! a brother? Nice little fellow, isn't he? Here! take this piece of pretty red silk for your patchwork, and run home, now. Tell your ma I'll be over to see her before night. I s'pose I *ought* to take her something to cheer her up, though I don't pity her one bit. If there's anything that I'm continually and everlastingly thankful about, it is that I've kept out of such scrapes.

Did you ever! if there ain't Miss Purson coming across the road, with that bunnit of hers in a newspaper, as usual. I've altered that bunnit once a year, and trimmed it twice a year, for the last—well, time out of mind! I do wish she'd get a new one; I'm tired of that Leghorn bunnit; it's like some people's tongues—there's no end to it. The first time she brought it, it was trimmed with plum-colored satin-ribbin and gold artificials, and I bleached it for her, and put the same trimmin's back on. I've sewed braid on to make it larger, and I've took braid off to make it smaller; It's been on the block more times 'an I've got fingers. I did hope she'd patternize me, and open her heart far enough to buy a new one out-and-out, this fall. I've a notion to tell her the straw's got so rotten it won't bear no more pressin'. Oh, good-morning, Miss Purson! Fine day! S'pose you've come to look at the new style of bunnits. Most all the gentility of Pennyville has been in to take a look and make their choices; but there's some left, that'll suit you, I guess, for all you're so insiduous. What! Thought you'd have your Tuscan bleached over and fixed up a little? Thought I told you, the last time, 'twould never stand another doin' over. I'd a great mind to charge you two shillin's extra, last fall, I had so much bother to keep it stuck together. If you want *that* thing teched again, you'd better take it to Miss Bungleby's shop; she'll be able to do it justice; and then she's so fashionable—gets her patterns after she has a good chance to steal mine, and puts *sech* an air on things! I think she'd make your old Tuscan look egregious. You'd like a new bunnit, if Mr. Purson could spare the money? Just tell him for me, that if he can't afford his wife a bunnit once in eight years, he'd better quit carpentering, and go to sawing wood; that he needn't aspire to the respectability of Pennyville any longer. Now, look here! here's a sweet thing—a Florence braid, with a lovely ruche, and all this bugle lace around the cape and brim, besides the feather. I showed it to Miss Grant, and she pronounced it superfluous. She said maybe she'd conclude to take it the next time she was in; but I hinted to her that it was spoken for, because I knew it would just suit your style and complexion, and I like to obleege my old customers. I asked her six and a half for it, but you may have it for six, seeing it's you, but I shan't make a cent on it.

Good Lord! if there ain't a buggy running away! do see how he kicks! he will certainly be thrown out! he's making straight for that pile of brick as he can go! I do wonder who it can be! It's a horse from the liberty-stable, and yes! goodness gracious! it's that handsome stranger that had that curly dog with the—oh, hevings! there he goes, smash-bang, right into the bricks! He's killed now, I do believe! I'm so scart, I don't know what I'm a saying. He's certainly killed! see him tearing down the streets, and the spokes a flying, and the poor young gentleman picking himself up. I must go to his assistance this minute. It shall never be said that Alvira Slimmens turned an unfortunate young man out of doors. Oh, sir! how do you feel? Are you faint-like? Lean upon me, upon my bo—shoulder. Dear me! I'm so flustered, I don't know what I'm doing or saying. Is it your head, or your arm, or your—limb? Ain't a bit hurt? only a trifle bruised? Thank the Lord! Well, walk in, and let me brush your coat. It's all brick dust. Can walk without assistance? Oh, I'm so glad of it! But don't over-exert yourself—don't!

Clara, Dora, get the brush! hand it to me. There, now, you look a little more like your present self. What a circumstantial escape you've had! I shall never cease to congratulate myself that the shop of Alvira Slimmens stood where it could afford a place of refuge to a ship-wracked stranger. Take a chair, won't you? My, your coat's tore out at the arm! Dora, bring a needle and some black silk. No, you needn't be afraid of making trouble. I'd rather mend it 'an not. Stopping long in Pennyville? Visiting, or stopping at the tavern? Oh, the tavern! On business I suppose? Any acquaintances? Ours is a very pedantic village, considered very rural on the outskirts, great deal of scenery and land around it. Perhaps you're an author, or an artist, come to rustify. I've read so many sweet stories about such things; and I declare, when you was thrown out in that terrible manner, I felt like flying to you, stranger as you was, and exclaiming, with that dear Moore:

"Come rest in this bosom, my own stricken deer,
Though the herd have fled from thee, thy home is still here."

Clara Browne, go in the other room this minute, and stay there till I recall you. What? *must* you go? Well, call again. I shall feel extremely solicitary about your health. Oh, no thanks at all, sir! I've only done my duty as one of my sex should do it.

He's gone. "Thou'rt gone from my sight,

like a beautiful dream!" How earnestly he kept looking back, as if he couldn't endure to tear himself away; but he must go to the liberty-stable, and let Smith know that his baulky horse has run away. If there ain't that sassy Clara, standing at the door, looking out after him, when I sent her in there because she kept making eyes at him, and laughing in her sleeve.

My hand trimbles so, I can hardly baste this silk on. It's come at last. I knew it would. I knew Alvira Slimmens was destined to see the hero of whom she has dreamed, about whom she has had many a ponderous fancy—that he would come in some unusual way; and now a circumstantial Providence has thrown him into that pile of brick, at her very feet, as it were.

Dora Adams, go over to Springle's, and get me a dozen of them new-fangled curling-clasps and a bottle of lavender-water; and let me tell you, once for all, that, if you and Clara don't quit a winking at each other, and making them secret signs, you'll repent it. [Murmurs *sotto voce*:]

"Oh, there are tones and looks that dart
An instant sunshine through the heart!"

and that was the way I felt. What a splendid subjeck for a poem for the "Eagle," to be called "The Runaway Buggy!" no! that's not romantic enough; "The Fearful Risk!" no! "The Stranger's Escape!" that's better; or, "The Castaway; or, the Leap for Life—a Tradegy," and sign it "Alvira S."—no! "A. S."—and send it to him. I'll do it this very night—write it while I'm putting my hair in papers. [Sings in an undertone:]

"Oh, Alvira Slimmens,
You'll soon quit bunnits and trimmin's,
Bunnits and trimmin's,
T-r-i-m-m-i-n's!"

CHAPTER III.

MISS SLIMMENS IS HONORED WITH A SERENADE.

FLY around, girls, and get this shop in a little better order! I'm expecting company, this morning, of a little genteeler order than usual. Them new-fangled curling-clasps are just the things. How's my ringlets? *I* think nobody could tell 'em from the most natural kind Anybody could tell, Clara Brown, that *your'n* had been in papers all night. I believe you're settin' your cap for somebody, or you wouldn't take all that trouble. Who be I expecting? Why, who should I expect, but the one that's the most likely to come? It's altogether probable that the common emotions of gratitude would prompt any right-minded young gentleman to testify his sentiments to his life-preserver. You wasn't aware that I had acted as life-preserver to any young gentleman? Well, if I didn't exactly

3

save the life of the stranger who was throwed out into them bricks yesterday, I did all I could toward it; and I offered him the refuge of my shop and of my—my support; and I dusted his clothes, and mended his coat, and made him fit to be seen again; and that's the next thing to it. If I was in his place, I'd sue the keeper of that liberty-stable for damages, and get enough to set up housekeeping with; though I suspect he's rich enough for that any time a day. He must be dreadful rich and aristocratic, he'd such an air, and his coat was cut so genteel. I almost wish he wasn't. I almost wish he was one of them suffering geniuses I've read about in tales, driven to the brink of separation by reduction in circumstances, and, jest as he was on the pint of committing death by suicide, *somebody*, some sympathetic being who had money laid up in the bank, would step forward, and rescue him from his suspending fate by the offer of her heart and hand and six hundred dollars in the Bank of Lowell.

Here, Dora, thread this needle for me. "Is my eyesight failing?" I'm not aware as it is, Miss Impudence—don't know any reason why it should. Anybody's hand would be a trifle un-stiddy that was all tremulous with expectancy, to say nothing of being up late last night, composing poetry on a certain harrowing event. Do I mean the marriage of Joshua Stebbins? Miss Adams! never mention that name to me again, unless you want to go home to your mother. I've told you several times that I give that man the mitten without any ceremony; and I'm gladder and gladder of it now than ever. I wouldn't have had him if his portcullis had been made of gold. Josh Stebbins! humph! the very name's enough! I wish I knew what *his* name was. He never thought to leave it. Of course, he's got one, unless he intends to appear synonymously; and even then he'd have to take a "nom de feather," as the French say. It isn't feather, it's plume? Well what's the difference betwixt a feather and a plume? I've not been a milliner for the last twen—seven years not to know what a feather is; and I don't ask to be taught by a miss that ought to be in her pantalets yet.

There! there's a knock! Wait a minute till I fix my hair a little. I wonder who it can be; I didn't see any one pass my window. Now, open the door. Oh, Miss Grant? how do you do? I was jest wishing you'd happen along.

Been a thinking about your folks for an hour back. How's your poor dear old grandmother—her rheumatiz is such an infliction—and the boys? I hear Reuben's going to start a singing-school as soon as cold weather and long evenings comes; and I hope the news is true, for I've been thinking of joining the school myself, as a powerful voice like mine that's used to church music is always a help to the rest; that is, if I'm a resident of Pennyville at that time, which maybe I shan't be. No, I don't know as I expect to set up the millinary business in any other spot; but I may take a fancy to quit it altogether. "Two yards of scarlet ribbon, wide"—here it is, if it suits you. It's for a sash, I reckon, to wear to the party that I hear is coming off next week. I sold that bunnit yesterday that you didn't exactly fancy. You said you thought you wouldn't take it; but I'm gettin' up another to be done against Sunday, that I shall try to have satisfactory; and I'll promise you not to make another like it for anybody in Pennyville. I'm not particular about the money till the end of the month; your fayther is always good pay. Did you hear of the dreadful accident? "No?" Is it possible? Yesterday—it was yesterday.

Oh, dear me! I haven't got over it yet! I expect you'll see an account of it in the "Eagle," when it comes out Saturday. No, they wasn't killed; but they come as near it as they could and hope to survive. You see, I was standing quietly in my shop, selling that very bunnit, and never dreaming of any trouble, and I heard a furious rattling down the street, and I run to the door, and there was the sweetest dark-eyed young gentleman that I never sot eyes on but once before, a stranger in the place, stopping at the tavern, coming dashing down the road as hard as he could kick, jumping and tearing like mad. I see in a minute 'twas that baulky horse from Smith's liberty-stable, and my heart riz up in my mouth, for he's an ugly creature; and there he was in such imminent danger, for he couldn't guide him at all, though he held on to the reins bravely, and kept his seat until he pitched for that brick heap across yonder; and then I screamed, for I give up all for lost; but, resolved I'd rescue him, or perish in the attempt, I ran right out in the road before the furious animal, throwed up my arms, and would have stopped him; but it was too late. He had smashed into the bricks, and the buggy upset;

and the gentleman was thrown into them head first; and I picked him up for dead. But, after I'd carried him into the house, and bathed his brow with camfire, and rubbed his hands, and unbuttoned his shirt-bosom to give him air, he survived, and, after awhile, was able to ascertain that he was not mortally killed. His coat was all torn to flinders. It took me two hours to darn it up, so that he could get back to the tavern with it. Five and sixpence for the ribbon; thank'ee; that's right. Tell your mother I've got some dress-caps now that ruther surpass anything I've had before. I sold two to Squire Waldron's wife, she liked 'em so well. Good-day. Come in to-morrow and get your bunnit.

Two o'clock! This is the longest day I've experienced for some time. Don't seem to be any business a doing, neither. I shall break up if things go on at this rate. What's that on the other side of the road? It's—no it ain't, either; it's only Jim Wilkins. Open the door, Dora. There's somebody knocking. Clara, my love, will you be so kind as to hand me—fiddlestick! what a scared-looking little thing! "Mother wants a skein of blue sewing-silk." Well, speak out, and don't stammer so. Here it is; though I don't see why you didn't go to the thread-and-needle store, and not bother me with your pennies. Alvira Slimmens is not so poverty-stricken yet as to be obleeged to sell a cent's worth o' silk. There, go along with you!

That's six times, if it's once, that Emmeline Jones has passed this window to-day. She ought to be ashamed of herself, gad, gadding about, and her poor mother at home, washing for a living! Perhaps she is going of errands? Pooh! perhaps she isn't. She's an idle, good-for-nothing girl, I make no doubt; sailing by in that old shawl as graceful as if she was a princess. She thinks those great black eyes of hers is going to save her the trouble of working for a living, as honest people have to. Some folks pretend she's got the consumption; and her mother makes a fool of her, nursing her up, and taking all the work on her own shoulders; but if there's any two things I can't abide, it's pride and laziness, 'specially when they go together. Some young girls not very far from where I'm sitting, may have some of the same notions, and the quicker they get rid of them the better, if they expect my patronage and support.

That's a queer looking wagon, going by. A

peddler's cart, most likely. He can't have tinware, or we would see it on the outside; it must be paper, or patent medicine, or furniture polish, or dry goods. And there goes a man, trotting by, as if he was going for the doctor, or running away from the hangman. And that just puts me in mind that I see a reward offered in a New York paper last week for the reprehension of a fellow who had been passing counterfeit money. That person that just passed looked like a counterfeiter. His whiskers was all over his face, and he had one of those wicked mustaches, and his cap was slouched over his eyes, and his horse was all in a foam, he'd been ridin' him so hard. What a curious coincidence it would be if this should be the same one!

Four o'clock! Well-l-l! it does seem as if the days were getting longer instead of shorter. It's an age since dinner-time. Good gracious! how that startled me! Go to the door, Clara. No, I haven't any paper—rags! Clear out, you little rascal! Here comes that begging Miss Burrows, with a subscription paper as usual. Good afternoon, Miss Burrows. Take a chair? No, I can't give a penny, and I won't! I don't make my own living now; the folks in Pennyville is getting too grand to patternize their own milliner, and going off to Lowell and Boston for their best things, and I shan't give one cent to any charitable purpose whatever, and I don't care if the minister himself hears me say so. I'm a-going to quit the sewin' society next week, and take my name off the Missionary Club. Charity begins to home. When Pennyville treats me as it oughter, then I'll treat it as I oughter. Only last week, Deacon Walden's wife come home with a velvet hat (*hat* 's the word now) that she paid nine dollars for in Boston.

Do hear that child squall! If Miss Peters is going to keep on raising a family, I'll move my shop out of this neighborhood. I've stood the screaming of nine successive babies, but I won't stand a tenth. You're doing your work all wrong, Dora. I won't pay you your wages this week, if you spoil that silk—and I really believe you have spoiled it. Clara Brown! you've done nothing to-day but start, and stare out that window, as if you were looking for a husband to happen along. You don't earn the salt to put in your porridge. If you wasn't seventeen years old I'd box your ears for the way you have put that border in. You needn't flush up, and shake back your hair so independent. You know very well that you've got no other place to go to; so you'd better take it easy. My! if the little baby isn't trying to cry! I hope she won't let her tears drop on that silk, because, if she does, she'll have to pay for the damage she's done. You're an ungrateful girl, Clara Brown, and I tell you, once for all——

Oh! how *do* you feel, to-day, Mr. ——? I believe I haven't the pleasure of knowing your name yet. "Mr. Wiggleby." Walk in, and take a chair, Mr. Wiggleby. Clara, dear, place a chair for Mr. Wiggleby. Dora, my love, take his hat and cane. We didn't *expect* to see you to-day, Mr. Wiggleby; especially as we feared that your injuries had proved more serious than was at first participated. Allow me to congratulate you upon your speedy restoration to convalescence. Oh, no! he! he! he! indeed, Mr. Wiggleby, I shan't take one particle of the credit upon myself. My humble efforts were prompted by the impulse of a woman's heart. You know what the poet says, Mr. Wiggleby? I know you do, now, and you needn't attempt to deny it. Those eyes and that forrid betray you to be one familiar with poetry as you are with your daily bread. But, as I was saying—

> "Oh, woman! in our hours of ease,
> Uncertain, coy, and hard to please,
> When pain and anguish wring the brow,
> A ministerial angel thou!"

That is the way with our sex, Mr. Wiggleby. If you had approached me in any ordinary manner, you would have found me "coy" and "hard to please," for I'm very bashful before gentlemen; but coming as you did, appealing to my tenderest emotions, when "pain and anguish wrung your brow," and your clothes was all covered with brickdust, and your coat tore, and I feared the worst—oh, sir, I shall never be able to express what I felt upon that peculiar occasion! I always felt as if some such thing was going to happen to me; and when it really took place, I was so flustered I never slept a wink last night.

But oh, Mr. Wiggleby! I shall never cease to remember, with burning blushes of diffidence and regret, the imprudence, the immodesty, I may say, into which my fright and overwhelming feelings induced me. *I* can never forget it, but I beg that *you* will; that you will banish it from your mind as a thing that has never been, or henceforth our future intercourse will be poisoned by the hateful thought that you are sometimes thinking of it, and condemning the act. "To what do I refer?" Oh, Mr. Wiggleby! is it *possible* that you were really insensible at that fearful moment? that you were not conscious that I received you in my arms? that your head was pillowed upon my troubled bosom? Then let the secret remain with me! you shall *never* know it, for Alvira Slimmens would *die* before she would willingly confess that a being of the opposite sex had reposed, even for a moment, upon her heart! much less, that in a moment of distraction, she had pressed her lips to his bleeding brow. I feel as if a mountain was lifted oft my breast, since I have ascertained that you are not aware of my indiscretion.

Clara, darling, you may go and see about preparing the tea. You will stay to tea, will you not, Mr. Wiggleby? We shall feel too much honored; and, indeed, we can't think of letting you go. There! I thought we could persuade you! Dora, I presume Clara will need your assistance. You can lay aside your work, and go and remain with her till supper is ready.

"What are the names of those young ladies?" You make me smile, for really I never think of them except as children; but they *are* growing up, I believe. Clara and Dora, two very pretty names; and they are nice enough girls, but foolish and giddy, like all apprentices. How do you like our village to-day? Have you perambulated about it sufficiently to be familiar with its principal inducements? I trust you will find charms to retain you here a number of weeks. It's so seldom we have a stranger among us, that he is quite a treat, especially to me, who feel *so much* the want of congenial, intelligent society among the young of my own age. Did you say you was a painter, Mr. Wiggleby? No? I thought perhaps you might be. What is your place of residing, when you are at home? Boston! Allow me to congratulate you upon being a citizen of the "Atkins of America," as our speaker said, at the last meeting of our Lyceum. You must attend our Lyceum, Mr. Wiggleby. We are quite proud of it. We have some excellent compositions, and some of the most instructive and exciting discussions. All our leading people take a part in it, including the minister and

Squire Grant; and there is an occasional poetical suffusion from—I won't say who. It's a great secret; and there's great curiosity among the young men to find out who their "talented and unknown contributor" is. You wouldn't guess it was me, now, would you, Mr. Wiggleby? I don't know that there's anything romantic in my appearance, but my ringlets and my pensive expression. Oh, now, you get out, Mr. Wiggleby! you're only trying to flatter me! *Would* you have known from the first glance that I was "a creature of the imagination, that there was but little that was real and substantial about me?" "She's all my fancy *painted* her"—how sweetly you quoted that, Mr. Wiggleby! Now, I'm *sure* you must be a poet. If you're fond of verses, I can read you some composed by a very dear friend of mine, no longer ago than last night, upon a certain subject interesting to both of us. I have them here; I just slipped them in my bosom to have them handy to look at, to remind me of the most thrilling incidents of my life. The authoress hasn't quite fixed upon a title-page yet, but thinks of calling it by some name that will be suggestive of the catastrophe.

After you've heard them, you'll be good enough, maybe, to give her the benefit of your taste. Hem! I hope you'll like 'em; hem-m!

The shades of night was falling fast,
As through the road to Pennyville passed—

(that's a poetical license about the shades, as it was quite early in the forenoon; but nobody expects poetry to be factitious)

A youth none ever saw before,
Whose furious steed pitched, plunged, and tore.
Whoa—oh! oh! oh!

His brow was sad; his eyes beneath
Flashed like a dagger in its sheath;
While like a clarionet loud rung
The accense of that unknown tongue—
Whoa—oh! oh! oh!

His hands were clinched about the rains,
The blood was freezing in his vains,
As, rattling over stump and stone,
Still from his lips escaped this groan:
Whoa—oh! oh! oh!

Attracted by the clattering noise,
The road swarmed full of men and boys.
Oh, "Stop him! stop him!" loud they call;
But he whirls out of sight of all.
Whoa—oh! oh! *oh!*

(Getting out of the sight of all is illustrious of the intense speed of his progress).

Alvira, by the sound amazed,
From out her window swiftly gazed;
She saw his danger; and her shriek
Told what she felt, but couldn't speak—
Whoa—oh! oh! *oh!*

Some twenty feet away, or more,
Almost before her very door,
Loomed up a mountain-pile of bricks,
Toward which, the wild steed runs and kicks.
Whoa—oh! oh! *oh!*

"Oh, stay!" Alvira cried, "and rest
Thy weary head upon this breast!"
She knew not what she did or said,
For love and pity turned her head.
Whoa—oh! oh! OH!

Wildly she rushed across the street,
That raging animal to meet,
"*My* life," she cried, "I'll give for *his!*"
And waved her arms, and shouted this:
Whoa—oh! *oh!* OH!

But madly on the pile he rushed;
The horse was hurt, the buggy crushed.
Half buried in the bricks she found
The youth, who bled from many a wound.
Whoa—oh! oh! oh!

There in the twilight, cold and grey,
Lifeless, but beautiful, he lay,
His hands in hers she wildly pressed,
And clasped him to her heaving breast.
Whoa—oh! oh! oh!

Her touch restored his sinking frame;
He gasped! he breathed! he sighed her name!

(Another license, as, of course, *at that time*, he didn't know it).

She bore him, living, to her shop,
While distant voices still cried: "Stop!
Whoa—oh! oh! oh!"

Do you *really* think it as pathetic as it is descriptive? My voice trembled so on the last verse I was afraid you couldn't understand it. Some envious people, who know nothing about authority, will be saying that it is not original, that I borrowed the idea from one of Longfellow's pieces; but I'll defy them to prove it. He *did* write something like it once; but who can prove which was written first, unless they know all the circumstances? And Longfellow is pretty well known to be a plagealizer. What! supper on the table a'ready? Well, girls, you've been uncommon quick this time. Walk out in t'other room, Mr. Wiggleby, and make yourself to home—to *home*, I say, because a young man stopping at a tavern must have a longing to hear the word once more.

Now he's gone, girls, I can tell you you had altogether too much to say to Mr. Wiggleby, considering that he was an entire stranger to you. "Children should be seen, and not heard," particularly at the table. I was mortified to death at you, Clara, when you came so near to spilling your tea right on the table-cloth with that everlasting giggling of yours. And—one thing more! let me tell you that I heard both of you laughing and stuffing your apurns in your mouth, with the door about an inch open, when I was reading them verses to Mr. Wiggleby. I didn't take notice of it at the time, as I hoped he didn't hear it; but you'll laugh behind somebody else's door, if you ever dare to play eavesdropper again. Go to bed, both of you! Do I want any help about dyeing my hair? When I do, I'll ask it. You'd better color your own, Miss Saucebox; it's getting redder than ever.

Hush! hark! that music is right under my window! Yes, Alvira Slimmens, as sure as you're a born woman, you're getting a serenade. I wonder what the neighbors 'll say now, with all their curling up their noses at you're being an old maid. How I wish I dared to raise the window! I would; but my hair is in papers, and my teeth are in the tumbler, and I've washed the paint all off my face, and my night-cap hasn't any ruffle to it, and my flannin bed-gown is anything but pretty; and it's so moonlight he could see the difference without a bit of difficulty. O my! ain't that heavenly? I *must* peep through the curtain a little. Yes, it's *him!* I knew it was! He's singing, now, and drumming on his catarrh. It's that sweet thing, "Will you meet me by moonlight alone?" Oh, I would gladly meet him, anywhere he said, that was proper, and folks wouldn't talk about! I'd meet him anyhow! I'd run away with him, if he'd only ask me. I'm going to tell him, next time he comes, that I own this house and shop, and have six hundred dollars in the Bank of Lowell, and perhaps he'll ask me to elope with him. Won't the people of Pennyville be astonished when they wake up some morning and find Alvira Slimmens has had a real, genuine runaway wedding? Dear! dear! how I wish I durst to raise the window, and throw him a bunch of artificials, seeing I've no other bouquet. I wouldn't mind the expense. I'm so afraid he'll think I don't heár. Hark! them forward chits are up, and are histing theirs—there! they've thrown down something, and he kisses it and puts it in his bosom. Of course, he thinks *I* threw it to him, and I'm glad they've done it; but they deserve to be shet up in a closet for their immodesty. How gracefully he leans against that post! He's the very picture of the Apollo Bellevue.. If he'd only stay long enough for me to take down my hair and put in my teeth, I'd answer him personally. But he's going; he pauses and looks back. Does he really want me to meet him in the grove at the end of the vale? To-morrow night, I'll sleep in my toilet, and then I'll be ready for anything that may happen. Dear! dear! nobody can tell what's going to happen, if they wait long enough.

CHAPTER IV.

MISS SLIMMENS MEETS WITH A VERY GREAT LOSS.

CLARA! Dora! come here both of you, this very minute! Where's my teeth? where's my teeth, I say? You don't know? Yes, you do know, too—you must! They're gone, and I can't find them anywhere in this room. I jest took them out, a few minutes ago, to brush 'em, and stepped out in the back yard for some water, and come in, and now they're nowhere to be seen. You needn't tell me they walk out of that tumbler without help. There's been nobody within gunshot but you two, and you're playing a trick on me. I'll have you both arrested—I will—marched off to jail, and kept on bread and water for a year. I'll swear you took 'em; for who else could? I'll go for the sheriff, now, this minute. Why don't I go? Yes, and meet Mr. Wiggleby at the very door, perhaps. He was to be here at two o'clock, to take me out a-riding, and it lacks but ten minutes of the hour, and here I am with my teeth gone. A pretty figure I shall cut, in this plight. Oh, girls, do help me hunt! Perhaps they've dropped somewhere, and I'm so distracted I can't see 'em. Do your best, and the one that finds 'em shall have a new silk dress, if she finds 'em before Mr. Wiggleby arrives. What's that? The tumbler was standing close to the window, and perhaps the cats got them, or some little boy has come into the yard and took 'em for fun? Oh-h-h! perhaps! I never was in such misery in my life. Them teeth cost me sixty dollars, hard cash! and to lose them—lose them *now*, of all times! I'd rather have lost my head. Hark! wasn't that the sound of buggy-wheels? Oh, I'm so glad it wasn't! I shouldn't wonder if that plaguy Peter's boy, Jim, had been hangin' around and seen 'em; he's up to all sorts of deviltry. Run over there, Dora, and inquire. Clara, have you searched under the bed? Dear! dear! dear! the clock has struck two. Oh, my teeth! my poor lost teeth!

What's that? my tears are washing all my paint off? Oh, you hedious girls! you'll be the death of me yet! How can you have the heart to make fun of me when I'm in such trouble? One thing is certain! if I ever do find out you've

had a hand in this, I'll be revenged—yes, revenged.

There! there's the sound of a carriage stopping! He's knocking at the door! Oh, dear! what shall I do? I'll throw myself on the bed, and pretend to be sick. I cannot see him, much as I want to; I look too frightful. Run, Clara, tell him I've been taken suddenly very ill, but I hope to be better by to-morrow, and will ride out with him then.

Has she gone, Dora? Oh, I dare not steal a look! I must hide my face in the pillow to stifle my groans. What's that, Clara Brown? Mr. Wiggleby regrets exceedingly his disappointment, but, since he has the carriage at the door, would ask permission to take *you* out a little while. You can't go, Clara; do you hear? If the jade isn't actually tying on her bonnet, and pretending not to hear! If I dared to step out and tell her, but he's standing right there; and I can't even forbid her. I'll bet a hundred dollars she heard me; and she'll have the impudence to say she didn't.

They've gone, and I've nothing to do but be wretched. Who knows what impression that saucy girl may have a chance to make? And I can't even go out to make good my loss. Oh, my unhappy teeth! Bless me, if they ain't lying right here on the bed! I believe I put 'em there myself; or else them girls have been playing me a trick. How I wish I could find out! I'd never forgive them to the lastest hour of my existence.

They're a mile way by this time, and I can set down to making .bunnits again, I suppose. And this was to have been the happiest day of my life! for I'm sure that I could have brought him to a positive declaration. I could kill that Clara Brown. The happiest day of my life, indeed! I could tear things, I'm so mad!

CHAPTER V.

SHE AGITATES THE QUESTION OF THE WEDDING TROUSSEAU.

RAIN! rain! rain! Do see how it drips down before the window, so a person can hardly tell who is who, that goes by! though there's not many people out *this* morning. I don't believe I shall have a customer to-day. If Mr. Wiggleby gets along, it'll be more than I expect; though I do think he is the devotedest of all the suitors I ever had. He's been perfectly intermittent in his attentions ever since I was the means, under Providence, of saving his life, and that's two weeks yesterday. I don't think the most envious creature in Pennyville, even Sally Meyers herself, can say *now* that I'm counting my chickens before they're hatched. If such civilities as Mr. Wiggleby has extended to me ain't paramount to a declaration, then I never received one. Six serenades, two buggy rides—besides the one I lost on account of mislaying my teeth—eight calls in the daytime and twelve in the evening, walking home by my side from church, in the presence of the whole congregation—why, any jury in the land, that had a spark of sentiment in its breast for the feminine sex, who had a wife, or a mother, or a daughter, or a sister whose heart it did not wish wantonly trifled with, would give me damages, in case Mr. Wiggleby should back out at this hour. But I'd rather have *him* than five thousand dollars without him; and I don't think he has the least idea of retreating. I think he grows more arduous at every interview. He squeezed my hand so respectfully, when he lifted me out of the buggy yesterday. I looked into his eyes to see if he meant anything, and he gave me *such* a glance! I declare I could hardly walk to the door without his assistance. What expressive eyes he's got, as black as this piece of crape and as bright as spangles, and such a pellucid smile in them. What convinces me more than anything else of the sincerity of his attentions is the frankness with which he has told me all about himself. It seems he came to Pennyville to do some law business for his father, who owns property out here about six miles—he showed it to me the last time we druv out together, and 'twas there he was going that time when Smith's baulky horse throwed him out, and he was borne into my shop, and recovered through my exertions—and he didn't expect to be retained more'n three or four days when he came here, but *business*, you know, is so prognosticating. He's been unavoidably delayed, he assures me, by occurrences which he didn't foresee. In short, he's found attractions in Pennyville that he had no idea existed here, and he don't know when he shall be able to tear himself away; he told me so himself. "Tear himself away," was the very words he used, and his manner spoke columns. Now, Clara Brown, what's your face so red for? and you're crumpling that lace all up, with your carelessness. I never see a girl change as you have the last two weeks; you seem not to know whether you're standing on your head or your feet, more'n half the time, and I've had to rip out and do over full three-quarters of your work. I'm thankful my trials in the apprentice line are pretty much over; for you'd better believe I'll shet up shop the day that I give up the name of Slimmens. I expect he'll build, maybe, on his father's property, and I've imitated pretty plain to him that I should have nigh on to a thousand dollars to help build and furnish the house with.

I want you girls to take hold and manage things a little more—take some of the responsibility on your own shoulders. If you do well and behave yourselves, there's no knowing but I may be induced to rent you the shop, and let you go along for yourselves. 'Tennyrate, I want you to take hold now, for I've got sewing of my own to do; I've sewed for other folks about long enough. I'm going to scallop the collar and cuffs of that night-gown I'm making, and put tape-trimming all around the edge; then I've ruffles to hem for three new night-caps, and some bands to stitch, and sew that knit lace on, that I did last winter in the evenings; I've my green silk to turn the skirt of, and, as soon as I can make up my mind what it shall be, I've another dress to make—a *party* dress, you know —he! he! I can't decide which to choose; whether to have a sweet white muslin, low in the neck and tucked to the waste, with white satin ribbin run in the tucks, and a sash of the same, or to have a pearl-colored silk and wear my bunnit. It's such an important moment of one's destination, it requires some reflection to decide upon so momentary a question. The bridal toilet is always the object of so much excruciating remark.

There goes Josh Stebbins out in the rain, with his umbrella over his head, and his wife following him to the door, to scold him for something he's forgotten, I make no doubt, or to ask him for something new, to make him draw down his stingy old face. I can see already that she's going to be very extravagant. There's groceries went into that house three times within a week, and a paper that I know was sugar every time; and they use three-quarters of a pound of butter every day of their lives, for I asked old Mrs. Grimes, that brings it to them, that day she was in here to see about having new strings to her black satin bunnit. I hope the children are well fed, since things must be wasted in such profusion. I don't believe the poor things are happy, and I've my reasons for it. The other day, I see little Jimmy standing out by the gate, looking so forlorn, and crying as if his heart was breaking; and I called him over, and gave him a cake with carraway-seeds and a lump of sugar, and asked him what was the matter with him—if he didn't like his new mother. You ought to have seen that child eat that cake! he never answered me till he'd swallowed it all down; and then he said he was crying because he lost the pretty new ball his mother made for him; but it's my opinion he was crying from hunger, and nothing else, though the poor little fellow didn't realize what was the matter with him. I asked him how he liked his new ma, and he said he liked her twenty bushels; and I asked him if she told him to say that, and that she'd shet him up in the closet if he didn't, when people asked him, and he acted as if he was afraid to tell me, but stammered, "He guessed so—he didn't know; his new ma had shet him up in the closet once when he was very naughty." My heart bled for him. I spread him a thick slice of bread, but he run off and wouldn't eat it. I've no doubt his step-mother has forbid him to stay anywhere long enough for the neighbors to find out how things is going. If she keeps anything that Alvira Slimmens doesn't worm out, either one way or another, she'll be the first inhabitant of Pennyville that's been deep enough to do it. Oh my! wouldn't I like to catch the first glance of Josh Stebbins' face, when he hears *the news!*

Rain! rain! rain! rain! just a purpose to keep Mr. Wiggleby away, and pervent Miss Grant from comin' to settle for that hat. It'll give my window a good washing, anyhow; and it needed it bad enough. Run, Dora, and get a towel, and tuck around the sash there where it's beatin' in.

Well, for the land sake, if there isn't Jonathan Grimes driving his ox-team in such a day as this! He's worn that old straw hat now going on five year. See how the water drips off, and runs down his back, and his long legs hanging down into the mud, and that red flannin shirt on! It's a mercy I didn't have *him*, if he *is* worth three thousand dollars, besides a part of the farm when his father dies. Did you ever hear how near we came to making a match, I and Jonathan? Oh, dear, I shall expire with laughing to think of it! It all came of that very old straw hat. You see, about those days, he used to look pretty spruce; though his legs always was rather long, and seemed to be in the way when he was setting down, or dancing, or standing still; though they was well enough in climbing fences and planting punkin-seeds; but he kept fixed up right smart, for he was paying attention to Joe Waters; and there was talk of their making a match. Most people called Joe very handsome; though *I* never could see much beauty about her, except her bright eyes, and her cheeks as red as pinys. In my opinion, she was right-down bold-looking with that dimple in her chin, and laughing whenever she got a chance. One day, he come in my shop, and he had that hat in his hand, which he had jest give two bushels of wheat for; and he wanted me to put a green silk lining in, and a good broad green ribbon around it. So I asked him to take a seat while I was doing the job; and he made himself very agreeable; and finally I laughed and said, said I, "I suppose you'll have another person besides Miss Slimmens to put the next lining in this hat for ye, if report says true, Mr. Grimes." And he blushed like a beet, and hemmed, and said, "he didn't know; he guessed not." And just that minute, as luck would have it, Josephine Waters appeared at the open door with a bunnit in her hand, which she had brought for me to trim with white. She looked kind of curious at us to see Jonathan blushing and me laughing;

and says I: "Oh, it's nothing, Joe! only I was accusing Mr. Grimes of being engaged to a certain somebody, and he was denying of it, as if everybody didn't know without being told. But la! he needn't have got so mad about it, seeing he's going to have the best-looking girl about Pennyville. It's no insult to couple that name with his'n, I reckon."

"I didn't know I got mad," said he; for he was a kind of bashful chap, and hadn't spunk enough to carry anything out.

"Well, maybe you didn't," said I; and then, to turn the subject, I asked him if he had heard of the rise of property in Pennyville since the railroad was talked of. "Why," said I, "four year ago I paid fifty dollars for this lot, and a hundred and fifty for the shop; and now I wouldn't take six hundred for 'em. I've a notion to draw my money from the bank, and spec'late in real estate."

"If you do, you'll make a pretty fortinate match for some man," said he, as he took his hat, and waited for Joe to do her errand. I see she begun to look grave, and her eyes flashed a little, for Joe was as poor as Job's turkey; and his folks had twitted her of it once or twice: but she told me what she wanted done to the bunnit, and then told me, very polite, that her mother was to have a quilting-bee to-morrow, and had told her to be sure and ask me. Then I laughed again, and said, "I'd be happy to attend, if I'd any way of getting there; but, as it was, I didn't see how I could, unless Mr. Grimes would volunteer to bring me in his father's new buggy;" and of course he couldn't get out of it, and said: "With the greatest willingness." And the two went away, looking daggers toward one another, with me laughing in my sleeve. I wanted to plague 'em, because I knew I was asked to the bee because I was the fastest quilter in Pennyville; and I'd heard of Joe saying that I painted; and I knew she stuck herself up on the strength of her good looks.

The next day, I was rigged out in my best, and the new buggy come to the door in grand style; and I was in such a good humor, that I got Jonathan to speaking out quite free, a thing even Joe couldn't do; and we was chatting away as merry as blackbirds when we drove up to Widow Waters'. Joe came out to the gate to show me in; and I spoke out just as she got within hearing, and says I, "No, indeed, it's too late now to break with *her*," just as if I didn't intend she should hear. Jonathan kind of looked confused, but wasn't quick enough to take, and let the matter slip. Joe got as white as a sheet, but smiled, and made herself agreeable to me; while Mr. Grimes drove off to stay away till tea-time. We quilted all the afternoon; and I saw she felt bad, and couldn't hardly make herself sociable with the visitors; while I was talking and joking all the time. During the evening, I stuck to her beau like a bur to a woollen stocking, and flattered him up so that his face shone like a punkin; and, when we went off together after that dashing horse in that new rockaway by moonlight, *I* knew that Joe was just ready to burst out a-crying; but *he* didn't, for she bid him good-night so gay, and laughed so loud, that the fool thought she was all right. It takes men a great while to learn how a woman will

> "Let congealment, like a worm in the mud,
> Prey on her damaged cheek."

What happened after that, I don't know, except that they kept up a coolness; and folks said the match was broken off. Jonathan began to call in at the shop occasionally; and I expect, if I'd a had him, he'd have married me. But his legs were too long; and he hadn't none of that romantic air which Mr. Wiggleby possesses in such an imminent degree. So one day, about six months after, when he came in to get a new ribbon, and said that he and Joe had made up, and was going to be married in two weeks, I told him "I thought they was a very good match, though the girl *was* poor, and her mother would likely be a dependence on him; and, seeing her heart was so set on him, I was glad *I* hadn't give him any more encouragement." I sent my most formidable compliments to the bride that was to be; and we've been on speaking terms ever since; though I don't think Mrs. Grimes has any love to spare.

They've got two young ones now; and I dare say she finds a farmer's wife has more work 'an play; while I, thank goodness, am still an independent candidate. There ain't a rag of her wedding finery left; while Alvira Slimmens is just indulging in the contemplation of what will become her best. Which do you think, girls—white muslin or pearl-colored silk? Dear me! what a delectable delight it is to the feminine sex to be engaged in deciding upon their bridal tournure! White muslin and a veil, or pear-colored silk and a bonnet? What a diploma to be in! Come, girls, say which you think will become *my style* best.

CHAPTER VI.

THE WINDOW IS CURTAINED (FIGURATIVELY) WITH CRAPE.

TEN o'clock in the morning, and those girls not here yet! This is the last time I let that Clara go home with Dora to sleep. I wouldn't have let 'em gone last night, but I expected Mr. Wiggleby was waiting for a chance to ask me to name the day; and if he'd wanted to stay and set up late, I didn't want them a-peeking through the keyhole. My plan was a complete failure, for he never come near me. Here I sot, fixed up to kill, till after ten o'clock, my heart vacillating wildly at every sound, and never a knock from nobody but them pestering Peterses, wanting to know if I had any pepper-mint, for the baby had the colic, as if *I* might be expected to keep baby-fixin's on hand! They'll be coming over to borrow "Mother's Relief," next; and now I feel as cross as a bear.

I'm tormented to know what kept him away; I never *did* feel so uneasy before, in all my experience. I shouldn't like to let anybody but him know how I have set my affections on that man. I've wanted to marry bad enough, though I've made a pint of pretending not to; but I haven't been *really in love* before, for years and years. The very squeak of his patent-leather boots, as he comes along the sidewalk, sets the blood a-flying into my face, and when he gets to the door, and smiles, and bows, and says, "Good morning, Miss Slimmens!" in that irreparable way of his, my sensations are inexpressible; actually, I haven't the strength, sometimes, to offer him a chair. He's my beau-ideal of a beautiful man. If he wasn't worth a cent, but was some nameless adventurer, or belonged to a band of fierce bandanas, or was a political exile with a price set on his head, or an unfortunate patriarch obliged to flee from his ancestral halls, it wouldn't make a bit of difference; there's something in the quirl of his moustache and the bituminous depths of his dark eyes that the soul of a romantic being of the softer sex cannot resist. I'd rather be his wife, and carry on the millinary business forever, than any of these Pennyville naps, and roll in luxury, and never be obliged to set a stich nor look at a fashionable plate.

Oh-h my! what a sigh that was! it come right up out of the pit of my stomach. I should *so* like to know what kept him away last night. I laid awake two hours, by the clock, thinking how I wished I wasn't more'n twenty or twenty-two, and had my own teeth and hair back again, and was a Mexican heiress, riding on a steed through a mountain pass, with only one servant for a protector, and a band of bandanas should rush out of a cave and seize me, and I'd struggle and pretend to want to get away, but should be overpowered, and my servant tied to a tree, and I shouldn't be able to help myself, but should be carried off in their arms into the interior of the cave, and should open my eyes, after fainting away in a graceful position, to find myself in a splendid chamber full of silver, and gold, and jewels, robbed from travellers, and find the chief of the bandanas kneeling before me, insuring me that if I would accept his heart and hand and marry him, I should come to no harm, and when I lifted my eyes to his face, behold it was Mr. Wiggleby, and I was impelled to wed him, whether or no!

I declare it makes me sick, to get up this morning and find this same old shop, and these same old bunnits, and my old sign a-swinging out there in the wind, after such a beautiful revelry. The millinary business was never intended for my destination, I'm convinced of that. If Mr. Wiggleby should come in here this hour and ask me to elope with him, I'd pack up my duds, draw my money from the bank, and do it. I do wish he'd come to terms, if he's a-going to. I feel that I've no time to spare, and I'm mighty uneasy about losing him; there isn't a girl in the village but would jump at the chance of becoming Mrs. Wiggleby. I've told him, point-blank, that I was worth three times what I am, for I knew it would be the only way to keep him, when there was plenty of "sweet seventeens" a-sighing for him. But I wish he'd *come to terms!* If there's anybody in the world that has had reason to realize that a "bird in the hand is worth two in the bush," it's me; and I wish Mr. Wiggleby was safe in my hand. I feel an unaccountable sinking of the spirits this morning.

Them girls aren't in sight yet. They won't find me in the best of humor; they'll have to have a better excuse than there's any danger of, if they escape my wrath this time. Half-past ten of a Monday, and they not here to begin work! Such conduct is unprecedental! The nearer they come to being of age, the more liberties they take. If I ever need their services, it's now. There's them eight Leghorns and three Dunstables to be hung in the bleach-barrel, and that bunnit I didn't get done Saturday, on account of going out a-riding with Mr. Wiggleby, to be sent home, and them children's flats to be lined and trimmed to-day, and I wanted to set down peaceably to my own sewing. The tape work isn't sewed on to that night-gown yet, and there's no telling how soon it'll be required. If he would happen along to apologize for not coming to keep Sunday night, I shouldn't mind their tardiness so much; but he isn't coming. I've looked up and down till my eyes ache, and that's all the good it's done.

I think that girl Clara has got altogether more vanity and pride than's good for her. What does she do but buy one of my prettiest white bunnits—a velvet one, with a plume—Saturday night, and pay for it out of her own purse. I didn't know she had saved up so much. She's set her cap for somebody, or she wouldn't have been guilty of such extravagance. I told her plainly I didn't think a velvit bunnit would be very suitable to her condition, and she said if she earned it and could pay for it, she didn't know who had a right to interfere; and then she tried it on and looked in the glass, and asked Dora if it wasn't sweet. I knew she was thinking all the time that a pretty bunnit made a certain pretty face look handsomer still; and when somebody knocked and Mr. Wiggleby walked in, I could have scratched her eyes out, she turned to him so saucy, with her cheeks all in a glow, and asked him how *he* liked her selection. She *did* look outrageously handsome just then; and I was on nettles till I'd thought of a way of taking her down by asking her how many weeks' wages, at seventy-five cents a week, it would take for a vain girl to buy a nine-dollar bunnit, and that I thought it would be very correspondent with a certain colored merino shawl.

'Leven o'clock! Well, this beats all! I'll put on my bunnit and go after them stay-aways in less than five minutes; and I'll tell Dora's mother if she doesn't keep 'em in better order, she needn't expect *I'll* do any more for 'em.

That's Dora now—no, it isn't—yes, it is; Dora Adams coming along alone, as slow as if she was marching to a funeral, and not a sign to be seen of Clara. I wonder what's that she's got in her hand, wrapped up in paper; and how she *dares* to take her time in this manner.

So, miss, you've got along, have you? Of course, you've an excellent excuse, something entirely satisfactory, for staying away till this hour, and putting the work back of a Monday morning. Where's Clara? Sick, I suppose, with cutting up of a Sabbath evening. What's that? You needn't stammer so, Dora Adams! You ain't stammering? Well, speak out, then. WHAT? "*Clara was married to Mr. Wiggleby at nine o'clock this morning, and hopes you'll forgive her for not finishing out her time, as her husband is willing to make it all right if there's any damages, and she sends her card and a piece of the wedding-cake, with their compliments!*" No, I never will forgive her—you know I never will, Dora Adams! Throw that wedding-cake out in the street—throw it out, I say!—and that card. I'll sue 'em both for damages! I'll sue her for her time, and him for a breach of promise. I'll break 'em up and ruin 'em, that I will! the deceitful, ungrateful, sly, tricky—hard-hearted — mendacious — outrageous—creatures! Hand me the camphire, quick! I'm swooning-oo-oon-ooning! The cam-phire!

Yes, I'm better now! Stand off! don't go to fussing over me with your pretence of being sorry! You've aided and abetted in this wicked conspiracy! I see it all now! No wonder I was overcome at the ingratitude of that serpent that I've nourished in my bosom, as it were, for the last three years! treated her as if she was my own sister, learnt her how to trim and do up bunnits in the best style, fitted her out to get her own living, and now she's rewarded my care and trouble by going off and getting married without so much as even asking my advice, and she with no mother to advise her, the bold, indelicate thing! to a perfect stranger, too. Flown from the protecting influences of my shop into the arms of a man! gone off with one of the male sex that she hasn't known over six weeks! How does she know but what he's got two or three wives already—but that he's a Brigham Young in disguise? I hope he is. I *hope* and *trust* she'll get come up with for her undecent behavior.

"You don't know as it's anything so unpardonable for a girl to get married, especially a poor girl, when she has a good chance?" No doubt you'd like to try the experiment yourself. How do you, or she, or anybody know that Mr. Wiggleby *is* a good chance? How do you know but what he's a runaway forger—I see one advertised not a month ago—or a gambler, or a contraband malefactor?

"Your mother wrote and ascertained all about him—that he was a most excellent young man?" Pretty business for a mother to be in! get up matches for other people! If she's upheld Clara Brown in this step to deceive and defraud me, do you go home to her, and tell her I've seen enough of you. Never do you darken my doors again, Dora Adams! I've had enough of prentice-girls bringing disgrace on my shop. There! you needn't flash up in that style! Isn't it a disgrace to have a young girl running off, and eloping with a stranger from the roof that sheltered her and the shop that learned her to bleach and trim, and the woman that took her in when she was a parentless orphan, with neither father nor mother? What's that? "I *did* take her in more ways than one!" Clear out, I say! go home to your mother, and run away with the first counterfitter that comes along. I thank Heaven I've kept out of *such* scrapes, if I have had my own way to make in the world! Go along with you! you needn't stop to look for your thimble. I'll send it home on a dray to your ladyship—hire a horse and cart a purpose. Go along, I say, and take in washing for a living, as your mother had to, before you came to me to eat and drink at my expense, and learn the trade of the best milliner in Pennyville. Not a word! I *won't* listen!

She's gone, and I'm "alone with my grief." Oh, Alvira, Alvira Slimmens! you built your house upon a sandy foundation, and now it's tumbled down, and buried your heart in its ruins. Didn't I *say* a bird in the hand was worth two in the bush? as I've proved to my own satisfaction long ago. I'll *never* forgive them! I'll ruin them, if it's in my power! I'll sue him for five thousand dollars, and bring his own wife in to prove his perjury. His *wife!* Oh, Wiggleby! Wiggleby! I allowed myself to lie awake, and dream that that term of endearment would be applied to me. I can't be so mad at you as I want to be. I ain't half so mad at you as I was at Joshua Stebbins; but I feel a good deal worse. I may jest as well give up, and be an old maid, and done with it. I'll never put my hair in papers again; and, if I didn't need 'em to eat with, I believe I'd sell my teeth. Crying? Yes, the tears is literarily washing the paint all into streaks on my cheeks; and I stand here before the glass, and see it, and don't care a straw. I never felt so completely used up before. I'm worse off than the old woman that was "cutting and contriving all day to get a nightcap out of a sheet." I've been cutting and contriving for twenty odd years to get a husband, and I hain't got one yet; and the material is all used up; and this last is the unkindest cut of all.

> "Oh, ever thus, from childhood's hour,
> I've seen my fondest hopes decay!
> I never loved a tree or flower,
> But 'twas the first to fade away;
> I never nursed a nice young man
> That from a runaway buggy fell,
> Binding his wounds as a woman can,
> But left, as soon as he got well."

I'll shet and lock the door! There shan't a customer get in this day! I'll lock the door and put down the curtain before the window, and take off my back-braid, and take out my teeth, and unlace my corset, and hang up my hoop, and go in my bedroom, and have a good comfortable cry!

CHAPTER VII.

JOSH STEBBINS'S WIFE'S FIRST TEA-PARTY.

GOOD-MORNING, Miss Peters; glad to see you out again, after your ninth. Take a chair and rest yourself. Let's see! it's nigh on to seven weeks old, ain't it? and this is the first time you've been in to see a neighbor. You've had sickness, and been pretty low this time. All I can say is, it's a mercy you ain't in your coffin, and Peters looking around for some woman to take care of his orphans. Thank'ee, I *don't* feel at all well. I've had trouble o' mind lately; them 'prentices of mine behaved so shamelessly, and I've had other troubles besides. There's nothing brings the wrinkles so quick as trepidations of the mind, Miss Peters. I shouldn't wonder if I looked as much as thirty years old, since Clara Browne played me that trick. I hadn't any heart to fix up any for several days, and I don't know what would have stirred me up to pick up my crumbs, but that invitation to a tea-party to Miss Stebbins's. I expected to see *you* there, as much as could be. Wasn't invited? Is it possible? There hasn't been no trouble, has there? I suppose it's because you've been sick ever since she come, and haven't called on her; but I don't think sh'd any business to be so particular, when she must a known it was because you wasn't able. She comes from a smaller town than Pennyville, and it don't become her to put on airs.

Well, I didn't feel like going out into company much, but I thought I'd go jest out of curiosity, to see what was to be seen; and la! I haven't been so amused in a long time. I believe I've always been considered as of an observatory disposition; I went a purpose to use my eyes and ears, and I used 'em. There's queer people in Pennyville, Miss Peters, very queer people; and anybody that's made a study of physiology, as I have, is apt to discover the peculiarities of their acquaintances. I felt myself very much improved by my visit; had several of my favorite theries conformed in an astonishing manner, especially my thery of oilyfactories—them's noses, I suppose you're aware—which I learned out of that highly useful and progressive paper, the "Laws of Life." This is an age of very progressive progress, Miss Peters, and I'm glad, for one, to have been permitted to exist during its continuance. Don't you find it so? Science are making gigantic strides toward some fulminating point of glory; physiognomy and electricity are running a race, to see which shall first reach the jail; the magnetical telegraph is stretching itself, like a boa-restricter, "across the bosom of the vasty deep;" and the comet is waving its flashing tail for hundreds and hundreds of miles in the hemisphere, giving astronomers an unparallaxed chance for stereoscopic views. But excuse me, Miss Peters; I didn't intend to touch upon these extended toptics when I began—my enthusiastic nature frequently makes me aggressive—and I'll come to the tea-party directly.

Well, I fixed up in my best, for one or two reasons of my own, principally to let Miss Stebbins see that Pennyville wasn't behind Salem Four-Corners in the fashions. I put four yards of the stiffest kind of bunnit-wire around the bottom of my hoop-petticoat, and put on six of the

"Laws of Life," gathered on a string, for a bustle, and I guess when I got there I took up about as much room as anybody. All the visitors admired my head-dress so much! I must show it to you. Isn't it sweet? There's a whole piece of narrow pink ribbon in it, besides the lace and artificials, and I was a whole evening putting it together. Well, I went early, to see everybody come in, which is half the fun of going to meeting or to a party. There was nobody arrived previous to me, except old Miss Grant, and she always goes at one o'clock in the afternoon. Miss Stebbins—have you seen her? she's a little thing, with a face like an apple and a form like a dumpling, no shape to her, no *style*—was dressed in a brown silk gownd, that I'll bet anything had been turned, and linen collar and undersleeves, to make people think she's equinomical, when the whole town knows she is spending Stebbins's hard earnings like water. Why, *I* could tell, the first time I seen her, the moment I looked at her oilyfactories—kinder broad and not exactly turned up, but just a-going to be—that she couldn't calkilate the difference between skim milk and cream. Stebbins's first wife used to make all her own butter, with that cow of theirs, and this un buys six pound a week, and gives the children the top of the milk for their dinners. Them children are fatting up beyond bounds, and 'll all look like their stepmother before spring. I wonder how she persuades *him* to let her go on so—he used to keep his first wife under his thumb till she didn't know whether her soul was her own or his'n. She must do it by coaxing, for nobody could ever drive Stebbins; and I think a woman that 'll coax a male creature that calls himself a man is in small business; *I* wouldn't make a fool of any of the selfish sex, by patting and petting him like a great baby.

As I said, there was nobody but old Miss Grant there when I arrived. Miss Stebbins was as pleasant as a basket of chips, said she believed Miss Slimmens and her husband were old friends, and she hoped I'd be as friendly with *her;* then, after we'd chatted a few minutes, she begged to be excused, saying she guessed she'd have time to mix her biscuits before anybody else come, and then 'twould be off her mind. I was just aching for a chance to get in her kitchen, to see how it looked; so I jumped up and said I wouldn't excuse her, but, if she'd excuse me, I'd keep her company; so we left old Miss Grant to her knitting, and I followed her into the pantry. Sich a kitchen and cupboard as that was! To be sure, it wasn't exactly dirty, but things wasn't in the order they used to be, and I wondered if they didn't ache to get back in the nice rows they used to be kept in. I never see any one with *that* kind of a nose that can know the meaning of the word order. But I will say there was plenty of nice victuals on the shelf, all dished, and ready to go on the table. I offered to set the table, while she was a-mixing up her biscuits, so as to get a good chance to peek around. I thought she didn't seem exactly willing, but she thanked me very polite, and couldn't refuse.

"It's something of a knack to make nice soda-biscuits," said I, as I set the honey and peach-preserves on the table.

"It is, indeed," said she; "it was a long time before I could get 'em to suit; but now, if there's anything I pride myself on, in the cooking line, it's soda-biscuits," said she. "I scarce ever make a mistake. Mr. Stebbins is very fond of 'em with honey."

"You might pride yourself on all your cooking, so far as that goes," says I, as I placed a beautiful pound-cake beside the preserves.

Jest then then there was a rap at the front door. Miss Stebbins had measured out her flour, her shortnin', and her milk, had mixed the cream tartar in the flour, and put the soda in the milk. "I'll have to wait before I make up the dough and roll it out," said she, "till it's time to put'em in the oven." And taking off her check apron, she told me to leave the rest of the table and come along and see who it was.

But I managed to stay behind a minute, putting the cheese on a plate, for an idea had come in my head to play her a little trick. If you'll promise on your word and honor, as true as you live and breathe, and keep the breath of life, not to betray me to nobody, Miss Peters, I'll tell you what I done, for the joke is too good to keep. I didn't do it out of any bad feeling, but just for the *fun* of the thing, you know; I always was fond of a practical joke, when nobody was really hurt. Of course, I *couldn't* have a spiteful feeling against Miss Stebbins, for she never did me any harm; and as I saw she had plenty of good light bread, I thought I'd take down her pride a little; so I jest stole into the pantry quick as a cat, and put an extra spoonful of soda in her milk, and was back in the setting-room in time to see Parson Higgins's wife come in, in that everlasting old purple silk of hers. She's smarted it up with new trimming —black velvet around the sleeves and cape. I always do notice her nose, but I noticed it then more than ever; it seems to get longer and sharper every time I look at it; just the kind that's always poking itself into other people's business—a thing, of all things, that I hate and despise! I have my faults, like other folks, but I thank goodness *that's* not one of them! It's been a mystery to me how Parson Higgins, meek as he is, has been able to sustain his place so long with a wife with them kind of oilyfactories; but I suppose its useful in sewing-circles and missionary meetings. It's a very efficient kind of a nose, if it isn't one of the handsome sort; them kind can turn out a great deal of work, and that's what's most wanted in a minister's wife. She and I never did agree very well, and since I've sent all my scraps of silk and satin to the other society, for pin-cushions, she's been as cool as a cucumber. We were uncommonly civil to each other, which is generally a sure sign that folks don't feel like hugging and kissing each other from love. Human nature is awful depraved, Miss Peters, and when two women is so dreadfully polite, it's a pretty sure symptom that there's some kind of hypercriticism going on behind it. We had scarcely got done paying our compliments and manifesting an interest in each other's health, when the rest of the company began to arrive pretty thick. Them two twin peas, Philista and Philistina Podd, made their appearance simultaneously together, as usual, both smiling like two cabbage-roses, both with red merino dresses on, both with black ribbons around their necks, pinned with cameo pins, both with two little water-curls on their cheeks, and black velvet streamers flying down their backs, and both said, "How do you do, Miss Stebbins?" in the same voice, at the same time, and both made a curchy at the same minute, and sat down together on the sofa. I don't believe it would be bigotry for one man to marry both them girls, for both of 'em together don't know as much as one ought to, and I defy Miss Sharp's spectacles to tell 'em apart. I may have my faults, but being like anybody else aint one of 'em, thank goodness! I don't intimate, and I can't be intimidated. Then there was Squire Waldon's wife, as fat and good-natured as ever, with her ribbons a-flying out like rainbows, and her face as red and as broad as the setting sun. She went round and shook hands with everybody, one at a time, asking 'em how their ma, and pa, and little brother, and darling sister was, and was *so* sorry when she heard anybody was sick, and gave so many directions about what they must do to get well, and was so intensely interested in Emeline Jane's cough, telling her to come round to-morrow and she'd give her a bottle of cherry pectoral, or some other stuff, and regretted so much to hear that Sally Thomas's grandfather had the rheumatism, and finally sat down by that tejus old Miss Grant, and got her to tell over all her ailments, from the sprain she got in her ankle, last winter, slipping on the ice, to the loss of appetite that had afflicted her since yesterday, till I was disgusted. Miss Waldon is a good soul as ever lived; the only trouble is, she's *too* good. She lets people lead her wherever they've a mind to; she gets imposed on, every day of her life, by somebody. I don't believe she ever turned a beggar away since she was a housekeeper, no matter how much of a flagrant he might be, without giving him something; and she believes everything that's told her, unless it's something bad about somebody. Every sick person in Pennyville, you'd think, was some relation of hers, she way she nurtures and sticks by them. As I said before, she's *too* good; it's tiresome to see a person so everlastingly good-natured. She has no discrimination; I can't respect a woman that's eternally getting taken in by every kind of a compositor. I've no doubt I've my failings, but lack of discrimination, I flatter myself, isn't one of 'em; her worst enemy can't accuse Alvira Slimmens of being easily made a fool of.

Did you *ever* see anybody dress in such hidjus taste as Miss Barker? I could hardly keep from holding up my hands when she came in, that afternoon! She'd made an extra effort to look fine, because Joe Taylor was expected in during the evening, to see the girls home, and she's set her cap for him in good earnest. Sich taste! you'd a died a-laughing when she made her depot into the room.

> "She wore a wreath o' roses
> On the night when first we met."

She had a wreath of silver artificials all around

her head, tied behind with a long blue ribbon. She's dreadful dark-complected, and blue's terrible unbecoming to her. You know how short and squatty she is? Well, she had on a hoop as big as mine, and a pea-green silk dress, that was

high in the neck, with a lace ruffle, making her look like a choked chicken around her throat; then she had orange-colored bows, all up and down the front, and a sash of the same, and her undersleeves was trimmed with red. She seemed as if she'd tried to see how humbly she could make herself look. If *I* had such outlandish taste as that, I'd commit death by suicide within a week.

But of all the creatures, I think the Widow Wilson bears away the palm-leaf! All she thinks of is getting married again, I know, jest as well as if I could see through her. Poor Wilson has only been in his grave three years, and a more devoted husband *I* never see than he was; his soul seemed sot on that young thing, that was nothing but a child at the best, and uncapable of depreciating his affection as it ought to be. I believe it was sinful for him to think so much of her—the reason he was taken away. All he lived for was "his Lizzie;" she used to set on his knee like an overgrown baby, with her white frocks on and her curls crisping around her neck; and now that he's gone and left her with plenty of property and everything to be comfortable with, she must go to casting reproach on his grave by looking out for another companion. What's that? "You've never seen her scarcely look up since his death, and out nowhere but to meeting?" You've thought her a poor, heart-broken little thing? Well, if you'd seen her day before yesterday, to the tea-party, you'd have altered your opinion. She come in as demure as a kitten, with her black frock, that she keeps on a purpose to contrast with her white neck, and sot down by the minister's wife, and had hardly a word to say to *us*, but when the *men* begun to come in, just before supper, she brightened up like a sun after a shower. What do you think she done? Jest as I'd got up to go and set by Mr. Hartly, the gentleman who's come as a partner in Squire Waldon's law-office, she flirted out of her seat on the other side of the room, and went and set down by his side, on the sofa, and commenced sich a close conversation with him, that none of us could get in a word edgewise; though he wanted to, bad enough, for he's an old bachelor of very agreeable manners, and, they say, the intellectualist person in Pennyville—that is, of the male sex. I'd just made up my mind to interrupt her, and give Mr. Hartly a chance to see there was some persons full as intelligent as Miss Wilson in our village, when Miss Stebbins come to the door to say that tea was ready—she'd been out the last half hour a preparing it. I saw she looked worried, and I surmised the reason. Mr. Stebbins seemed surprised at the flustered look on her face, which had been so mighty pleasant before she went out; but when we all filed into the dining-room and took our places at the table, and he lifted the plate of biscuits to pass 'em around, the mystery was explained. He looked at her so inquiring and mortified-like, that I thought she would burst right out a-crying, for, you see, this was her first attempt at entertaining company, and she's a childish thing, anyhow. Such biscuits you never saw! as green as grass in streaks, and smelling of saleratus enough to drive a person out of the room. "I don't see how I come to make such a mistake," said she, in a distressed voice; "I never did before. The company will have to make out on bread, for they cannot eat my biscuits, I'm afraid."

"Young housekeepers is liable to mistakes," said Miss Waldon, soothingly, "and your bread is excellent, good enough for the queen; so don't fret a minute about your failure, Miss Stebbins—pray, don't!"

"She's always hit it to a T, before," said Stebbins, oneasily.

"I guess it was because I tried *too* hard," said

his wife, trying to smile; "still, I can't account for it. I'm positive the measure was correct."

"'Tain't worth speaking about, Miss Stebbins," said I, ready to burst with laughing, secretly, to see her pitiful face. "We've all eat worse many a time, and anybody that can't make out a meal on what you've sot before 'em ought to go hungry. I suppose you find Joshua a little particular, on account of having such a superior cook for his first wife; but 'time works wonders,' and I've no doubt you'll make out very well after a while."

I'm afraid she'll find me rather a sorry comforter, for she didn't really rally the whole of the rest of the evening; but as for me, I was in excellent spirits at the success of my innocent little joke, especially as I had a seat next to Mr. Hartly, and kept by him pretty much of the time after we left the table. I'd made up my mind to impel him to see me home, just to spite that Widow Wilson—not that I cared anything about him, for this was the first of our acquaintance—but the forward thing got the start of me, and carried him off before my eyes. It takes them widows to come around the men. A young lady like myself would be ashamed to practise sich arts as they resort to. I'm not perfect, no more'n some others, but hypocrisy and artifice isn't one of my faults, thank gracious! I do think a designing widow one of the most shameless of the female sex.

What! must you be going? I'm *real* sorry you wasn't to the party; Miss Stebbins *ought* to have invited you, though I suppose you couldn't have gone if she had. Do bring that sweet little darling of yours over with you, the next time you come! I dote on babies, especially on your'n, Miss Peters, they're all such little loves!

CHAPTER VIII.

AN "ARGOS-EYED" SPIDER WEAVES A WEB FOR A FLY.

THERE goes Lizzie Wilson, stealing by in her deep mourning; you'd think her face was as melancholy as her garments, if you didn't see it all in a glow, like a young girl's. I wonder where she can be going this forenoon, so early! into Martin's store, I'll bet, to buy something pretty to set off her face. Like as not, she's going to put on second mourning, to imitate to a certain person that she doesn't feel so afflicted as she did a while ago. No! she's gone by the store; and now—yes, as sure I'm here, peeking through this curtain, she's gone into Squire Waldon's office. Well, if *that* isn't carrying matters on pretty boldly, I wouldn't say so! What a blessing it is my window looks up and down the street so far, and over that other road that crosses it, too. I should miss some rich sights, if it wasn't for this window. Squire Waldon isn't in his office, for I see him drive away in his buggy half an hour ago. Of course she'll come right out, when she finds he ain't there; for any woman must know it would be highly improper for her to remain alone with an unmarried man in his office, even on business—which it isn't likely she has any. I'll bet anything she knew the squire was out, and took this opportunity to visit Mr. Hartly alone. I'm going to set here with my work and keep watch how long she stays. It's half-past nine now by the clock. I feel so ugly since Clara Brown went away, I'm just aching to give somebody Jessie! Speaking of Clara, I expect it would be policy in me to tell Dora Adams she can come back to the shop. I hear she's promised to go to Miss Fudge's, and if I make an enemy of her, she may tell some things I'd rather have kept. 'Tennyrate, I don't want her to go over to Miss Fudge's side! that woman has been trying to get start of me, ever since she come to Pennyville and set up her opposition to an old-established shop like mine. Dora must be kept away from *her;* I'll go over to her mother's this evening, and tell 'em I've made up my mind to forgive and forget the past, and do the best I can by her, if she'll be as good a girl as she used to be. Dora's such an easy-tempered little thing, she'll come back in a minute; and I must say she's better taste than anybody in this village, myself excepting. I find it quite too hard, getting along without her handy fingers; besides, I don't feel so mad at her as I did before I made the acquaintance of Mr. Hartly. Perhaps it's all for the best that Mr. Wiggleby fell in love with Clara Brown. Goodness alive! there he is now! My heart is right up in my mouth! It's the first time I've sot eyes on him since he came back from his bridal tower. He *is* a handsome man, that's undeniable; but he's not so much dignity as Mr. Hartly, and I don't feel never so much overcome as I thought I should.

Ten minutes by the clock, and Widow Wilson hasn't stirred out of that office yet! She must have set down to a regular flirtation, for any ordinary business could have been enacted in less time than that. Here comes Miss Belden after her cap-border. I hope she won't stay long, for I don't care to lose sight of that office-door. I'm bound to see *who* submerges from it, and *when!*

Good morning, Miss Belden! Come for your cap-border? I've got it all ready pinned up in paper; it's only fifty cents. I'm in an awful hurry this morning; never was in such a flurry in my life! Both my 'prentices is gone, you know, and I've everything to do myself right in the busiest season of the year. You'll excuse my talking much, for when my fingers flies so fast I must keep my mouth shet. I've seven orders to finish by Saturday night. Don't go! you can set as long as you like, if you'll excuse my keeping on with my work. Well, if you must, you must, I suppose. Good bye. Run in again, soon.

A good riddance! Seventeen minutes by the clock! Aha, Widow Wilson! you don't guess who's keeping an eye on your proceedings! You think your widow's weeds are going to give you impunity from remark, when they're all the more reason why a woman should deport herself discreetly.

Twenty minutes! I'm perfectly scandalized by such conduct!

Twenty-three minutes, and no signs of that black dress intruding itself from that door yet!

Twenty-seven minutes by the clock!

Thirty minutes, and there she comes! Now, if any one can explain what business could keep an unprotected female, and a widow, a full half-hour in a lawyer's office, all alone with an unmarried man, they may do it to their own satisfaction, but they can't to mine! I'm fur from being of a suspicious disposition—I never believe anything bad of anybody till it's *proved*—but what a person sees with their own eyes, and counts by the clock, they are excusable for believing. Here she comes! tripping by with a face as innocent as the day. That face might deceive an angel of light, but it can't Alvira Slimmens. Now I don't really think there's anything wrong between her and Mr. Hartly, but she's trying to catch him, and has invented some excuse for going to see the squire, to get a chance to make an impression, and that's as great a crime in my eyes as any she could be guilty of. She's had one husband, and now she'd better stand back and let other folks have their chance! I won't put up with her interference. She'll hear of this adventure before a week is out; I'll bet my head on that. Some people in Pennyville have found out before this there's a pair of Argos eyes in it that can see in more directions than one; and if a married woman and a widow cannot exercise any more prudence than she has, she must suffer the consequences; I shan't hold myself responsible.

Here comes Mehitable Green. She's the sharpest nose in the village; it always gets into my shop some time before its owner is visible. As Campbell's Minstrels says: "Coming events cast their shadows before," and I'm awful afraid, always, when she's in here, that she'll knock down some of my fancy articles with that prognostic of her'n. It's better at scenting out a precious piece of scandal than a pig's snout is at rooting out chestnuts. I'll put a flea in her ear before she gets through with her visit, that'll do the business for Widow Wilson; and that without running any particular risk myself.

La! Mehitable Green, is that you? Come right in, do! You're the very person, of all my friends and acquaintances, I was the most wishing to see. I've been so busy lately, I've had no chance to hear the news, and of course you can post me all up about Pennyville sayings and doings. Sich a favorite as you be in the community must know pretty much all that's a-stir-ring. Set down, and we'll have a good, old-fashioned chat.

By the by, did you meet Miss Wilson just before you got here? She just passed by here on her way from Squire Waldon's office. The squire has gone to the country; so I suppose she and Mr. Hartly must have had a nice, quiet visit, seeing she stayed the bigger part of the forenoon with him. Hey? Oh, I don't know; *business*, of course! These widows with property always have plenty of business to enact with all the marriageable lawyers that come in their way! Don't you wish you and I had some sich good excuse for making a two hours' visit all alone on Mr. Hartly? not but that it's perfectly proper—Lizzie Wilson never does anything but the very properest—and I wouldn't say it wasn't for the world. *Of course* she had important law matters, or she wouldn't have stayed so long—especially in that private office where Mr. Hartly keeps his desk and books! No, I don't say it! I don't say anything, Miss Green! and I wouldn't have you mention this little concurrence on no account. Miss Wilson and I are good friends; and if I *knew* anything bad about her,

I wouldn't say it. You must promise me on your word and sacred honor not to speak of this little affair; for it *may* turn out not to mean anything. I'd hate to put a wrong construction upon anybody, let alone such a pink of propriety as Miss Wilson. What, already? why, you've hardly set long enough to get rested, and I did want a good long set-down with you. *Be sure*, now, not to speak of what has passed between us; I've told it in the strictest confidence, because I know if I could rely upon any one's voracity, it would be Mehitable Green's.

CHAPTER IX.

WANTED, A WIFE: MISS SLIMMENS ANSWERS THE ADVERTISEMENT.

HAND me that paper, Dora, that come around Miss Tuttle's bunnit. It's a Boston paper, and has got the latest news, probably. If it should have one of Longfellow's sweet, dear poems in it, I should want to cut it out and paste it in my scrapbook. I idolize that man! his poetry is so mellifluent, and his sentiments always congeal with my own. I've ever regretted that it has been our fate not to meet. If we'd have met in time, the destiny of Alvira Slimmens might have been very different from the fashionable milliner of Pennyville. I feel it within me, that I am not all that I was culpable of. I do hope there's some more of that "Aristocrat of the Breakfast-Table" in here. I want to find out if that forward chit of a schoolma'am is going to succeed in her arts and endeavors, which

I can see through as plain as a millstone, and should think he might.

Next to the murders and elopements, I always read the deaths and marriages—not that I know the people, but it's so exciting!—and next the advertisements. Bless my stars! Well, did you ever! (*Reads*):

"MATRIMONIAL.—A young gentleman, a student of Cambridge, who has graduated, and is now pursuing the study of the law, is desirous of opening a correspondence with some young lady, with a view to matrimony. She must be young and tolerably good-looking, not entirely destitute of fortune, of an amiable disposition, and possess a large share of the sensibility and enthusiasm which makes the gentler sex so charming. He would prefer a lady of poetic temperament, though not by any means a *blue-stocking*, vivacious, witty, and with good musical taste. The advertiser offers, in return for requiring so much, youth, health, an ardent, impulsive heart—quite new, having only seen service some three or four times—good prospects in his profession—being said to possess unusual talents for the law—a handsome form and face, with a particularly killing moustache, a romantic mind, and agreeable manners. Any young lady answering to the above description, and worth not less than three thousand dollars, with which to pay a few debts contracted at college and set up a sweet little suburban establishment, yclept 'love in a cottage,' will be sure of receiving the most candid treatment, and of finding a husband in every way calculated to make her happy. Address, with stamp to pay return postage, ADONIS, Cambridge, Massachusetts."

Dora, go and light the brimstun under the bleach-barrel. (*Soliloquizes:*) I'll answer his advertisement this very evening. How fortunate that I picked up that are paper! I might never have known how near I had come to what I was wanting, and missed. I'm the very person to suit him, in every particular. If I'm not exactly *young*, I can make him think I am, by the application of paints and emetics, and plenty of ringlets and ribbons. He describes my temperature as well as if he knew me—"sensitive and enthusiastic"—and I flatter myself I can lead in the choir about as strong as any woman in Parson Higgins's meeting-house, so far as music is concerned. I don't just like that paying up of his debts, though I presume they don't amount to over eighteen or twenty dollars for candy and cigars, which all young gentlemen must have, and I'm arriving at an age when it will be necessary for me to make *some* sacrifices to get a young, good-looking husband. Oh, my! my heart vacillates at the bare prospect. If there's anything I admire in a man, it's an arduous disposition, such as he confesses to, and I always have thought I should take to them Cambric students, they're so dashing and just a little bit wild. What's the use of my slaving and toiling in this shop for the last twenty years, if I can't enjoy my money, now it's made? Only to think of a suburban residence, all nestled down in roses and marigolds, and such a sweet air of delusion about it, and me a waiting for my husband to come home to tea, like a wife that Mr. Irving tells about, whose husband met with a reserve of fortune, and my Adonis coming up the revenue, while I stood on the porch watching for the first glimpse of his lovely mustache breaking through the distant foliage like—like anything. Oh, it's too good to be true! I'm afraid he won't love me; but then, as he is in such want of funds, which, no doubt, his father sternly denies him, but he will give him plenty by and by, maybe he'll take me, if I *am* over twenty; and when I once get him under my thumb, trust Alvira Slimmens for pulling his hair if he don't behave! He'll have to be a good boy, if he gets pin-money out of my pocket. I'll engage to manage him after the ceremony is once said.

Got that brimstun to smoking, Dora? Well, run up to the stationary store, and bring me a sheet of pink letter-paper and a pink wrapper to correspond with it—the best he's got—and two postage-stamps, and get him to make me a good pen, with a fine p'int, oil-boiled. And oh! don't forget a stick of blue sealing-wax; and remember to tell him the *best* paper he's got; I'd prefer it with some problematical device, like a Cupid flying, or a rosebud, or two doves with their bills entertwined, or something similar. Stay! you might as well get three sheets of paper and three wrappers, as it's likely I shall want as much as that in the course of events.

You can go to bed, Dora; it's half-past eight—time children was abed. I've a little writing to do, and wish to be left to the solitude of my own meditations while I'm a rolling up my hair.

She's gone off giggling, the little minx. I'd have kept her at work an hour yet, if I hadn't been aching all day to get at that letter. It'll take me till midnight to compose it. Now everybody's gone, and the street is quiet, and my hair in papers, and my corset's unlaced, I feel just in the mood. I'll write it down on a piece of foolscap first, and copy it out fair and square. Let me see! how shall I begin?

Dear sir. No, that's not romantic enough; everybody begins that way. My dearest Adonis; that's two affectionate for the first, it'll do better for the second. Let's see! Unknown but admired Adonis. Unknown but congenial. Unknown but kindred-souled; *that's* the very touch!

"UNKNOWN BUT KINDRED-SOULED ADONIS: I have read your advertisement in a Boston paper. It has made an impression upon me for which I cannot account. Suffice it to say that, after long resisting the inclinations—through motives of feminine delicacy, which ever prompts the true of my sex to 'blush unseen,' as the poet says—I have found it impossible longer to withstand what is evidently my destiny. 'Fate cannot be controlled,' says Byron, who is one of my favorite authors. Tell me, is he not also yours? But you need not answer; I *know he is!* The same initiation which tells me what your spirit is destined to be to mine tells me this. Is it not curious? But thus it is with those who were created for one another. It seems to me as if we were already intimately acquainted, as if I had poured out into your soul the burning—but pardon me! my enthusiastic temperature is carrying me away from the dictates of that modesty which is my idol. Dear Adonis—there! 'from the fullness of the heart the mouth speaketh,' and I don't want to waste time by throwing away this letter, so again I beg you to pardon the arduous impulse of a youthful mind—it seems to me as if I must have seen you somewhere; perhaps it was only in my dreams. Your description of yourself is my exact ideal of a sweet young man, the very portrait which has ever slumbered in my breast. Dare I hope that mine will be so satisfactory? I am twenty-five—a little older than you hope for, am I not?—but my affections are virgin; they have been sacredly cherished until I should meet the hero of my musings; and with one of my arduous and romantic mind and exhuberent disposition, a few years, more or less, will make no difference. My lips have never yet been pressed by mortal man; I have kept the inferior youths of this vicinity at a proper distance. I am not positively handsome—my mirror tells me that—but I am *called* intellectual-looking, have long, flowing ringlets, that curl naturally and impart an air of childish grace to my otherwise almost too dignified demeanor; my cheeks are of a lovely red, I have hazel eyes—enviable people call them grey; but all the poets have grey eyes, you know:

> 'Eyes of grey—
> The soft grey of the brooding dove'—

and with my figure I must say I do not think you will be displeased. I have ever loved poetry and the contemplation of the sublime and gorgeous in nature. Although I do not profess to be a poetess, my emotions often impel me to the composition of verses on my favorite subjects. I inclose 'An Ode to the Moon,' which was an entirely impromtu suffusion, which I wrote by moonlight one evening during the past summer, and which was published synonymously in the 'Pennyville Eagle,' and much admired.

My disposition is gay and infantile, but not so flippacious as that of many young ladies of the present day. Last and least—for of course young people of such sentiments as you and I are more or less indifferent to peculiary considerations—I have the sum you mention, three thousand dollars, in my own right, unincumbered, though not all cash. My property consists in a dwelling and lot, which can be readily sold, as it is in the centre of a flourishing village, part of the stock of a flourishing fancy and millinery establishment, and a thousand dollars in the Jewell Bank. If we suit each other, as my spiriticious perceptions insures me we shall, I shall not object to paying up in full such small debts as your youthful indiscreetness may have incurred. As to the 'love in a cottage,' it suits my tendencies so well that I shall be willing to sell out my Pennyville property and invest the amount in a sweet, deluded retreat, somewhere amid the 'classical shades' of Bostin, which I have always longed for—the intellectual privileges of its inhabitants. Hoping that your heart will respond to the sentiments which oscillate in mine, and that you will appoint a personal meeting soon, I shall look unintermittingly for your reply to this. When could you appoint our first interview, and at what spot? Let it be soon. With mingled sensations of anticipation, your *spirit bride*,

"ALVIRA SLIMMENS.

"P.S.—I send you three postage-stamps.

"P.S.—If you require peculiary aid to enable you to visit this region of the country, let me know the amount. Do not be modest.

"P.S.—Alvira cannot rest until she hears further from *her* Adonis!"

CHAPTER X.

SHE IS ACCUSED OF SCANDAL.

AH! Mr. Hartly, how *do* you do? Walk in and take a seat. I'd begun to give up all hopes of the honor of a call from you. Pleasant weather for October, isn't it?—quite balmy. I guess we're getting our Injun summer, that delightful season which our aboriginal bards appear to be so fond of. I remember Longfellow speaks of it. Do let me take your hat—*do!* How do you like our village, Mr. Hartly? I suppose you begin to feel to home here, by this time. Find the people unusually well-informed for a rustaceous neighborhood, don't you? I hope you'll make up your mind to reside here as a permanent residence. We shall hate to give you up, now that we have found out what a treasure you are. Gone into partnership with the squire, I reckon? What's that? Come to call on business? he! he! The female sex are not supposed to know much of such affairs, unless they chance to be of a pragmatical turn. But what is it, Mr. Hartly? I am curious to know.

WHAT! Miss Wilson has got out a warrant against me for label, and you have come to serve it? Ain't you ashamed of yourself, to pass yourself off for a gentleman, and come to take advantage of an unprotected female in that way, Mr. Hartly? A label! I never said a word against Elizabeth Wilson in my life, never, and nobody can prove that I ever did! What damages does she sue for? "A thousand dollars!" Well, I hope she may get it. These things has got to be *proved*, Mr. Hartly, and I defy anybody to prove 'em. Where's her witnesses? What does she say I said? When did I say it? Tell her to prove it, I say; tell her to prove it! I *ain't* excited, but I'd like to know what I'm accused of saying, and who's her testimony. "Miss Wilson was very much grieved and hurt to hear, some days ago, that she was the subject of false and outrageous stories, which were being circulated through the village!" Well, what was them stories? "That she'd been known to spend the whole forenoon in your private office, alone with you, and had been seen coming out of it just before daylight, three mornings in succession!" That beats the pigs. And who says *I* said it? "Miss Wilson has taken the trouble to trace them carefully, and has found that they all come from Mehitable Green, who will swear in court that she had it every word from me?"—from me, Alvira Slimmens, who was never known to say a bad word about anybody, as long as she's lived in the village of Pennyville! That Mehitable Green is a perfiduous wretch! I never said one word of it! I don't remember as I ever mentioned Miss Wilson's name to her, for, if there's a person in this village that everybody is impelled to respect, and never find nothing to say about her, unless it's what's good, it's Elizabeth Wilson; and if there's a person in this village that I wouldn't breathe a secret to, if I had one to breathe, it's that Mehitable Green. Why, she's known as a scandalizer and a labeller, from Dan to Behemoth! I'd like to see her, and see if she'd tell me, to my face, I said it! She dursn't say it to my face, bold and pernicious as she is? She's said it herself, and she ought to be held responsible; SHE ought to pay damages!

A thousand dollars! Why, it would break me up, root and branch, after all my saving, and working, and accumulating in the millinery line! Seriously, now, you're joking, ain't you, Mr. Hartly!

There she goes, now, scringing along without coming in, as if she was afeard to meet me! I'll call her in! Mehitable! Mehitable Green! come in here a minit.

So, Mehitable Green, I've gone, and done, and been a-saying things about Miss Wilson, have I? Oh, you needn't deny you've laid the sin at my door! Here's Mr. Hartly, who's going to take your deputation that you're so anxious to give. Now, then, out with it! What did I say about Miss Wilson? "I said I'd seen her coming out of Mr. Hartly's office before daylight, three days in succession!" Mehitable Green, I'll tear your eyes out, if you ever say that again! It's a perfiduous, malicious, base, and unprovoked falsehood, and you know it! Let me at her! don't retain me, Mr. Hartly! I want to scratch her face for her. Well, it ain't very becoming, that's a fact, sir, but I've had more provocation than I can bear. Don't go yet, sir. I'll be calm and collective, if you'll remain and hear it out.

"I did say, anyhow, that she was in the habit

of spending her forenoons, when Squire Waldon was out, alone with his pardner, in his private room?" Will you take your Bible oath of that, Mehitable Green? You'll have to swear to this in court. *Insinuated* it, did I? Ha! ha! we're coming to the point, Mr. Hartly. "I *did* say I see her making a two hours' visit on him, in his back office, the other morning, and that I supposed she'd make a good excuse for it!" Well, that's a *little* nearer the truth than you've teched before. Come to think of it, the last time Miss Green was in here, Miss Wilson had just passed by, coming from your office, and I spoke as she passed, and said she must have some law business to do, as she'd been in the squire's office the last twenty minutes, and that I'd no doubt it was important business, as she had considerable property to 'tend to. That's the long and the short of the whole matter, Mr. Hartly, and if Miss Wilson feels hurt about it, I'm willing to apologize, though of course I can't make any subtraction, as I only stated a simple fact, without the least bad intention.

Oh, yes, Miss Green, I've no doubt you're sorry you *misunderstood* me, now that the shoe is on the right foot, and the right person is in danger of damages for label. If you're sorry, you'd better go to Miss Wilson and say so; perhaps she'll forgive you, and perhaps she won't. *I* intend to see her before to-morrow morning, for if there's a person in this village it would distress me to have a falling out with, it's Lizzie Wilson, who's as sweet as she is handsome, and as good as she is sweet. I hope, Mr. Hartly, you haven't such a poor opinion of me as to think I could injure an angel like her, and an unprotected female, like myself, with no one to defend her from the slanders of the world. Good-afternoon, sir. Give my love to Lizzie, and tell her I'll call and make it satisfactory to her. *Good*-afternoon, Miss Green.

Good gracious, but I was scared when he made known his errand! That Mehitable hasn't half the sense I give her credit for. I'd no idea she'd carry the matter so far, and make herself liable to the law. If she'd had any prudence or wit about her, she could have done as I done—*hinted* things so darkly, nobody could have fixed anything upon her; but a person that's born a fool can't help themselves, I suppose. The fat came pretty near being all in the fire. It would have been terrible unfortunate for my correspondent to come on here and hear that I was in danger of losing my thousand dollars through a suit for label; and he's to be here this very evening. Oh, my! my heart's right in my mouth all the time. Eight o'clock this evening is the eventful hour! I've sent Dora home to her mother, and slicked up the shop, and now I've nothing to do for four mortal hours, but to do these curls over on the curling-tongs, put a little more carmine on my cheeks, dress up in my pink silk and lace cape, and set and anticipate. I *do* hope the stage won't tip over, or any accident happen. I shall be fidgeted to death with suspense, if he's not punctual to the minit. I wonder if he'll see how old I really am. I intend to have the lamp pretty dull, and use plenty of emetics.

Dear me! I hope that five-dollar bill I sent him will be enough to meet his expenses in coming. How frank it was of him to ask me for it, and what a stingy old father he must have, to keep such a nice young man on such a short allowance. It's very liberal of him to expect only three thousand dollars in a partner, when he'll be heir to thirty thousand when his parent dies. It proves that he isn't mercendary in his character. I can't abide pursemoney in a man.

Dear! dear! how slow that clock ticks! It

never was so dilutory before. I'll see how I look now I'm attired. It's hard to pass the time with only one's own reflections. How are you, Miss Slimmens? I must say you're looking your best; you've done your cheeks and eyebrows beautifully. I shouldn't wonder if you took him in. Do your best, Alvira; you'll never have another chance.

Wasn't that the gate? I wish I durst peak through the curtain. No, not him yet. I'll put a little perfumery on my lips, and chew these cinnamon-drops, for he *may* wish to salute me, which would be proper, considering our relations. There! it's HIM!

CHAPTER XI.

SHE IS EDIFIED BY THE THANKSGIVING SERMON.

THIS is a sweet day for Thanksgiving; the sky's as blue as indigo! I was very much edified by Parson Higgins's sermon this morning. You ought to have went, Dora, instead of spending the time flirting around, as I've no doubt you did. He's a powerful preacher, the parson is, when he's a mind to. His subject, this forenoon, was charity; he divided it into nine heads, and every one of 'em was worth listening to. *Some* people inside of the meeting-house must have felt hit, if they'd a particle of conscience left. I declare I don't see how he dared be so personal, as I knew he was. I should have thought them that the coat fitted would have got awful mad. He said there was other kind of charities than giving things away to the poor; he said that backbiters, slanderers, and evil-speakers must all of them answer for their want of charity—that putting wrong constructions on people, and getting up trouble in families and churches, and always looking on the dark side of things, was a great and a crying sin. I declare, he might have just as well spoke Miss Sharp's name and Mehitable Green's right out! He described 'em exactly; and I couldn't help looking over to see how they took it. I expected to see their faces as red as fire, with a guilty conscience; but la! they were looking as cool and unconcerned as could be, and that Miss Sharp was turning her head to look at *me*, when she ought to be hanging it for shame. But when the parson said that some folks took credit to themselves for being very benevolent and all that, because they ground the faces of the poor in secret, and put a penny in the contribution-platter in public, I jest wanted to smile, for I knew *everybody* must apply it to Miss Tucker, who always heads the missionary paper with fifty cents, and who pays her washerwoman in cold victuals and old clothes. Why, I heerd from somebody that had it from the woman herself, that the last time she washed there—and she had such a big washing she never got done till seven in the evening, and her three children waiting at home for their suppers, poor things! —she asked Miss Tucker for a little money, for that once, as she wanted some very much to buy her some wood with; but Miss Tucker said she could get plenty to do it without paying cash; however, as she'd had a hard day's work she'd pay her nice and liberal in what would be better than money; so she gave her a little bag with nigh about a peck of corn-meal in it, and a ham-bone, and a two-quart basin of broken victuals, and a great bundle of old clothes to make over for the children. So, when Miss Smith got home, she kindled a fire with some sticks she'd picked up on the way, and put the pot over, and made a good lot of mush, for the young ones was hungry, having went without their dinners; and when it was done, the meal turned out to be so awful sour and musty that the children cried and said it was nasty, and wouldn't have touched it, if they hadn't been half starved. There wasn't meat enough on the ham-bone for a dog to pick; and as for the rest of the stuff, it was just fit for the swill-pail—*I* guess it come out of it. So after she'd got the young ones to bed, she thought she'd look over the bundle, and see if she could find something to run up a frock for Mary before she went to sleep, for the child needed it dreadfully; and would you believe it? there wasn't a rag in the whole mess fit for anything but paper-rags. She said they wasn't worth the thread and the time she'd have to put in the rotten old duds. The whole stuff she brought home wasn't worth twenty-five cents, and she'd done full six shillings' worth of washing. I wonder if Miss Tucker didn't think of *that*, when the minister was speaking.

Who's that? Open the door, Dora. No! clear out, you begging little brat you! I've got no old shoes nor nothing else to spare. Oh, yes! "father's drunk and mother's dead!" they always are. Shet the door, Dora; I'm cold, with that air rushing in here a perfect stream. Didn't I see you giving that little beggar a three-cent piece? Don't ever do that again, encouraging the little thieves to come around my shop. No doubt, he was an impostor. He'd have stole that piece of crape there, if he could have reached it, when our eyes was turned. I believe in giving to the poor, when you've anything to spare, but not to these street beggars; they're *all* impostors, every one of 'em! I *might* have given him that pair of blue woollen stockings that I said I'd never darn again, his toes stuck out so, if I'd believed the little rascal, but I didn't; besides, I've saved them stockings to give to that old woman that does my scrubbing for me. She's thankful to get anything! It's a real charity to give her work; and she's willing to take most anything in pay she's so bad off. Dear! dear! *I'd* have got right up and walked out of church, if the minister had hit me as plainly as he did Miss Tucker.

"Charity doth not behave itself unseemly," said Parson Higgins, and I know he was thinking of Miss Grant and them Podd girls. Did you *ever* see girls take on so, as them Podds do?—so fond of the gentlemen! Anybody could see they are crazy to get married; and the way they giggle, and blush, and flirt round on the very church steps, to say nothing of their parading themselves past Jim Miller's store every day of their lives. There they go, now, in their pea-green merinoes and pink bunnits, sailing by, making an errand, I'll warrant you, at the store, to buy a row of pins, as like as not. I should think, after the reproof they got from their minister, they might stay in the house for *one* day.

"Charity is not puffed up." I believe Parson Higgins looked straight at Miss Dawson's new bunnit and velvet cloak when he said that. She's getting so mighty fine she can't put up with Pennyville fashions. She sent off to Lowell to get her bunnit, instid of patternizing me, as she used to. I'm glad he give her a hit. That impudent Miss Sharp nodded over to me, as much as to say he was a-hinting at my marabout feather and white terry velvet; but if a milliner can't afford an occasional good bunnit who can?

I declare, the minister didn't spare people's faults, and he hadn't ought to; it's a preacher's place to warn and instruct his perishingers. If he'd a hit *me*, I should have said just the same. It was as good as a play to me, to set and see people squirm that had their toes trod on.

I guess Miss Green felt mean about all she'd said to injure Miss Wilson. I do believe she wanted to catch Mr. Hartly herself. I don't see any other reason for her slanders and the trouble she made.

There goes the parson and his wife now, on their way to Squire Lawson's to dinner. I expected to be invited to meet them myself.

Mrs. Lawson must be getting rather stingy in her invitations. Howsomever, I couldn't go, for I'm expecting company myself to tea, a *friend of mine*, from Boston, the same who called here last evening, when you was home. You may set the table, Dora, and start the fire in the kitchen stove, and put that chicken on I picked this morning, and the tea-kittle. Put some peach-perserves on the table, and that cake you baked for me yesterday, and a mince-pie, and them biscuits. When you've got everything done, you can run home and spend the rest of the day with your mother. I *would* ask you to stay to supper, but I know it would be more of a treat to you to be to home, and you can take one of them pies, and a bowlful of that quince-sass, and that other fowl, as a present from me to your mother. If there's anything else you want, take it, for I'd like to feel you'd just as good a meal as I have. The Lord has been very merciful to me this year, and I don't want to be stingy of his bounties. I feel to thank him for all his providencies, especially his throwing that Boston paper in my way. I've reasons that you don't know of, Dora, but will soon, for regarding it as the most circumstantial providence that ever occurred to me.

Don't you be too curious, and you'll know all before a week.

I haven't seen any one going to Peters's to dinner. I don't believe they've asked a soul out of their own family; and with nine young ones to feed, I shouldn't think they'd want to.

There's a whole carriage-load of folks drove up to Stebbins's. Run, Dora, come here! Do you know any of 'em? Neither do I. It must be her relations, coming to keep Thanksgiving. They're some of 'em there the most of the time. It must go rather against the grain with that stingy Stebbins. Serves him right! needn't have married a woman who brought him nothing but an army of relations. Do see how she flies out the door, and hugs and kisses 'em! Hope her soda biscuits will be as good as they were the night I was there to tea. People call her a *good cook!* Why, them biscuits was as green as grass and as heavy as lead. Thank the Lord, Stebbins got the wool pulled over his eyes that time. There's Stebbins himself come out, now, and purtending to be so tickled, laughing and shaking hands; but he needn't purtend. *I* know that man better'n most folks do, and I know he is sorry for some things he didn't do, as well as for some he did; but it's too late for repentance, and *I* shan't be the one to say he isn't as happy as he might be. If he could have got the woman he wanted, he'd have been a different man.

Hurry up, Dora, or you won't get home in time to cook that fowl for your supper. I want an hour or two for quiet retrospection before my company arrives. A mediative mind like mine is always fond of solicitude and reflection. I shouldn't ever write any poetry, if I didn't indulge in these reverential moods. I really believe I could compose a piece this afternoon, if I wasn't agitated by anticipatory sensations. Besides, as it's Thanksgiving, I suppose it will be perfectly approbious for me to sing a few hymns. I don't know when I've felt the approbiousness of a hymn as I did one of them that was sung this morning. When I reflected upon what might have been and what was to be, upon the past, the fearful past, and the future, the transcending future, upon Clara Browne's running away and my picking up that Boston paper, I felt my heart pouring out in the lines—

"Judge not the Lord by feeble sense,
But trust Him for his grace;
Behind a frowning Providence,
He hides a smiling face."

Since I come home, I've composed and added these few lines:

"There's better fish within the sea
Than ever yet was caught;
The Lord has spread thy net for thee,
Then trust Him as thou ought.

"He filled the fishers' nets of old,
Do thou prepare the bait,
Nor let thy faith and hope grow cold,
Alvira, work and wait!"

CHAPTER XII.

THE NIGHT BEFORE THE WEDDING.

UNROLL that bundle, Dora, and see what I bought *you* this morning, when I was a-buying for myself. Ten yards of real Swiss, lace for the sleeves, and a whole piece of blue lutestring ribbon for the sash and tucks. Do you know what for? Well, that dress has got to be made and fitted by to-morrow night, and you've got to wear it and *stand for my bridesmaid!* I knew you'd be surprised. It's rather sudden, but you know I always *was* a believer in "love at first sight;" and when two persons of contiguous sentiments meet, and feel that each has met the pardner of their destination, that they are unanimous in every respect, what's the use of putting it off? As my sweet Adonis—that's his synonymous name, Dora—says, "there's no use; let us not tremble on the verge of bliss, but plunge instantaneously into the thrilling fountain of happiness! Let us no longer remain apart—we who have been too long strangers upon the same globe, yearning for each other, yet dissatisfied, we knew not why—knew not until we met, and then the mystery was revealed. Let us become one in the eyes of the tonsorious world, even as in spirit we are!" Those were his very words, Dora. Are they not beautiful? How could I persist against such winning persuasions? I could not! I named the day, and to-morrow is the day! To-morrow, at eight o'clock in the evening, Alvira Slimmens will be submerged in a new capacity.

I've had but a short time to mature my plans; but I think I shall leave you in the care of the shop at present, and all the profits of the work to be yours; and if that uncle that you spoke of, that might help you to buy out the stock, comes forward with two hundred cash down, I'll let you have the shop, with good time for your payments. Come! measure off that skirt, and run up the breadths; there's no spare time; yet the time seems endless to me, when I reflect that I shall not see him again until an hour before the ceremony is to be performed. He's gone back to Boston to perfect his arrangements. Oh, Dora, if you could see him! He's as handsome as a picture, and the sweetest black eyes, and such a lovely scarf and clothes, and a ring on his finger, and his hands as small and white as a woman's, and do you know I fancy he resembles Byron, or, at least, Byron's Corsair! I never expected to be so superelatively happy! Wasn't it fortunate I trimmed up them caps and things just before Clara Brown run away? They're all ready for an emergency, and I've nothing to do but get this dress made and pack my trunks. See! how do you like it? I'd a sent to Lowell, but I hadn't time; and this is next to what I wanted. I *wanted* a white more-antic, but there wasn't a yard in Pennyville, and I considered myself fortunate in finding this silver brocade. I paid three dollars a yard for it, at Curtis's; but a person don't get married every day, 'specially to a beautiful young student, that writes poetry and talks the dead languages as fluidly as his mother's tongue. Hand me them scissors, Dora. Dear me, I'm so flurried, I'm afraid I shall spoil the set of it. Won't you pull my corset-laces a little tighter, till I fit on the lining?

Make your frock as pretty as you can, for the

ceremony is *going to be in church!* I'm determined all Pennyville shall have a chance of seeing that Alvira Slimmens hasn't gone through the woods to put up with a crooked stick at last —not she? Mehitable Green will burst with envy, to say nothing of them twin peas, Philista and Philistina Podd. I've heard of their remarks. I guess somebody hasn't been any worse off for a chance to get married than they have; and if they don't feel spiteful when they see the bridegroom, then I miss my guess. There's nobody in Pennyville that will begin to compare with him. Clara Brown-that-was's husband couldn't hold a candle to my Adonis.

Snip that down a little lower in front. There! how does that set? You see, it all come of my reading the advertisements. He advertised in that Boston paper, all about the kind of a wife he wanted, and we've been holding an episculatory correspondence ever since. He's been to see me twice, and we were mutually fascinated. The only fault I can find with him is, he's almost *too* pressing. He was determined I should set the very earliest day I could, and overcome all my scruples with the persuadingest eloquence, which I could not possibly resist.

When you come to Boston *to buy your millinary goods*, Dora, you must come and see us. We are going to live in the subbubs, in the sweetest spot; he's described it all to me—a little rustaceous abode—a nest, he called it, a nest for his dove!—half cot, half villain, in the Gothic style of archetype, standing in the midst of a lawn, empowdered in trees, a fountain gambling in the mist, a portcullis running round three sides, the road to Boston just visible, here and there, through the intricacies of the foliage, roses twisted round the pillows, and such a cunning little China padoga in the back garden! He's gone to purchase it now. That's the business which keeps him from my side; otherwise, he assures me, he would not forsake me for an hour—that is, so but that he still haunted the vicinity of my abode—till *we were one!* He's placed the most touching confidence in me, as regarding all his peculiary affairs. I know just what his expectations from his stern old father are, who keeps him on short allowance till he shall settle down into a prudent, stiddy, married man. He's going to pay down five hundred on the cottage, and lay out two hundred more on the furniture, which is to be in readiness, with a cook in the kitchen, and the tea-table set out, on our arrival at *our home*, when we have completed our bridal tower. Isn't it romantic? I was so pleased with the picture he drew, just like a novel, of our arriving at home at the twilight hour, with the lamp lighted in the parlor, and the servant opening the door to the new master and mistress, that I drew him a check for seven hundred dollars, to get everything ready beforehand, though I hadn't calculated at first on laying out so much until everything was sure. What's that? You should have thought I would have been afraid to trust a stranger? Me and Adonis strangers! What a ludicrous idea, Dora! It's plain you don't appreciate our spirituous relations; nobody but a kindred spirit could. We've been acquainted millions of ages, in some other spear, Adonis says, and I believe him. To be sure, I can't exactly recollect, but when he asked me if I had not some dim foreboding of the shadowy past, if I had not always felt a want never before satisfied, if I had not seen his features in my dreams, I answered, yes; and when he pressed me closer, and wanted to know if that had not been the undefinable reason why I had rejected all my previous suitors, I told him that it had

Oh, Dora, if you'd seen how delighted he looked when I gave him that assurance, you wouldn't wonder at my bliss. His face beamed with a soft smile,

> "Like a light within an alabaster vase,"

as Tom Moore says, and he folded up the check for seven hundred dollars on the Lowell Bank as carelessly as a piece of newspaper, and put it in his pocket-book

> "With a gesture full of grace,"

and squeezed my hands and looked into my eyes. Oh, Dora! He placed this ring on my finger, as an outward testimony of our engagement. It's a real diamond, of the first water. Every time it sparkles it puts me in mind of what's coming; not that I ever forget it for an instant, but it seems more *bone fido.* I was afraid he would be displeased when he learned I had accumulated my money in the millinary business; but it didn't seem to make a bit of difference with him; he laughed, and said so nicely that a "bottle of frangiponi would remove all the odor of Boquet de Brimstone from these precious fingers·" and then he put the ring on the engagement finger, and kissed it, and I felt in the seventh heaven of rapturous sensation.

See if you can hook up this lining. I'll hold my breath—now! Oh no, it's not a bit too tight. It's going to make up sweetly, isn't it? I stopped at Mother Brush's on my way along, and engaged her to bake me two nice loaves of cake, one of them to be the wedding-loaf. I'm going to have cake, and wine, and confectionary, and after the ceremony such of my acquaintances as I invite are to stop in and congratulate us. The notes are to be sent out in the morning. Won't there be a flutter in Pennyville?—he! he! I think I see Mehitable Green reading hers. I've asked her and Miss Sharp on purpose to see how dumfounded and enviable they will be. Won't I be polite and dreadfully civil when Miss Green comes up to wish me joy!

Eight o'clock, a-ready! One day more! twenty-four hours of "maiden meditation, fancy free," and Alvira Slimmens will be no more. I don't know where the time has flew to. My dress is hardly two-thirds done; and to-morrow I shall have all my packing, and my dressing, and a thousand little things to do. We won't get to bed before midnight, Dora. Your frock is going to be charming. Blue is very becoming to your fair complexion. I must stop sewing long enough to put my hair in papers. I don't know but it's fortunate that my Adonis is going to be absent all day to-morrow; 'cause I can leave my hair rolled up till the last thing, and needn't be bothered with rigging up, till I dress for the ceremony.

Nine o'clock! I'm glad there's an hour less. Dora, hand me that trimming for the sleeves.

Ten o'clock! Twenty-two long hours still left!

'Leven o'clock! Heigh-ho! I wonder if he's asleep.

Twelve! *The wedding-dress is done!* Come, Dora, go to bed

One o'clock! for the last time!

Two! I wish I could compose myself to slumber.

Three! I hope the stage won't be delayed, or tip over!

Four o'clock! Will morning *never* get here?

Five! I hope he doesn't sn-o-r-r-r-e! rr-r-e! r-h-h-r e!

CHAPTER XIII.

THE WAY IT TURNED OUT.

SIX o'clock, and he's to be here at seven! Oh, Dora! I shall never get dressed in the world, I'm so successfully flustrated. Hurry on your own things, and be ready to help me when I get my hair out of papers. Is that cake sliced, and the wine on the server, and the plates and glasses and everything in order? I leave it all to you; for if I should be looking right straight at 'em, I couldn't tell whether they was there or not.

These curls are beautiful; they never looked better. If they'd been fruzzy now, or the weather had been wet, and straightened 'em out! I guess Pennyville has been in a stew to-day, if it never was before. Dear! dear! there's only one thing lacking to my peace of mind, and that's the capability of looking into the houses, and seeing the effects of those little notes with doves on them, that went fluttering around this morning, like feathers, and lodging in people's domινces. I'll warrant this has been as long a day to some others I might mention as it has to the bride-intended; some others whose curiosity was their leading trait, and who're dying this blessed minit for eight o'clock to see how the bride is dressed, and what for a looking person, Adonis de Mountfort, Esq., the bridegroom, is.

Do see how the men are gathering about the door of the tavern, down the street there, where the stage is expected to stop! Dark as it is, I can count more'n twenty. They're there to see him get out of the stage when he arrives. Lordy! but wouldn't Miss Sharp like to go over there and look on, too, if she durst to?

Yes, you're all right! looking sweetly. Did you tell your beau to be over to the tavern to escort Mr. de Mountfort here, and to be all ready to transact his part as groomsman? How's my checks? I want 'em just a little red, you know, but rather pale. Brides are always rather pale, you know; 'specially when they're young and sensitive. Oh, Dora, if you should ever be in my situation, you'll know what my feelings are!

Don't let me forget anything, particularly my handkerchief, for I shall probably shed a few tears, and want something to hold to my eyes. I expect to be very much affected; but I don't intend to faint, if I can help it, as I might be liable to disarrange my bridal tounare.

Mercy! how the time does keep running on! Hand me my dress. I must say this is the most opprobious dress for a wedding that was ever got up in Pennyville, if I do say it, that made it myself.

Can you see the sextant going over to the meeting-house yet? O yes! he's lighting up a'ready. My, I must set down a minute! it gives me such a realizing sense of what is about to take place, I am completely overcome. Lighting the bridal lamps for Alvira Slimmens at last! thank goodness!

There! I guess I shall survive in a short time. You may hook me up. Ugh! that was something of a squeeze, wasn't it! *Now for the orange wreath and bridal veil!*

They're on, and I am ready! Do you see the stage yet?

Seven o'clock. The hour for his arrival has arrived! I wish it wasn't so dark out, we might see if the stage has drove up yet. I thought I heard wheels several minutes ago. Now that I'm all ready and waiting, I feel terribly. I shall be all in a trimble after a few more moments of suspension. I don't know what to do to calm myself, unless I read over his last sweet letter. Dora, child, be sure you don't make any blunders to spoil the effect. I want the ceremony to produce the greatest sensation of anything that has ever transferred in Pennyville. I hope Mr. Ellis has studied *his* part thoroughly. If they get here in season, we must practise a little before we start to church.

A quarter to eight, and no signs of his arrival! O Adonis! I hope, I trust no accident has occurred. I feel that I could not bear it, after being wrought up to such a state of expectancy.

Only five minutes to the time! Everybody in the church, and waiting—I can see them in my mind's eye—and no bridegroom yet. The stage must be upset, or some terrible accident. Pour me out a glass of that wine, Dora, and then throw your shawl around and go and inquire if there's any news of the coach. *You must!* I shall expire if this suspension continues much longer. My curls, too, are beginning to come out, and it's blowing up, as if it was going to rain. What will the folks think to be kept waiting in this style! I've a presentiment of some awful occurrence. There! thank goodness! that's the gate! they're coming! Open the door, child, while I compose myself.

Oh, Mr. Ellis, is that you! Where is he? where's Mr. de Mountfort? has the stage arrived? is he coming? What keeps him? Perhaps it's to change his clothes, and the coach was later than usual. Oh, Lord 'a-mercy! What do you say, John? "The stage came in an hour ago, and he wasn't in it!" Wasn't in it! Don't tell me so, don't! He's sick—he's dead—he's false! No! no! he *isn't* false—never! I will not say it; I will not think it; he's dead! I know he is. O dear me! oh-h!

Take away the camphire! I don't want it; he may come yet, by private conveyance. Do you think I'm going into church to be married smelling of camphire? How late has it got to be? Half-past eight! O dear! what *will* the congregation think? Mehitable Green is beginning to turn up her nose, I know she is! I can't bear it; I can't bear it, I say! anything but that—oh-h!

Oh, Mr. Ellis, won't you go to the telegraph office and see if there isn't a message for me? I shall expire long before morning, if I don't hear from him to-night. There's a knock!

Only the post-boy! but he's got a letter; let me see it. "Boston!"

John Ellis, go to the meeting-house and tell the minister and the people that the marriage is postponed—that Mr. de Mountfort is very sick, and couldn't get here to keep his appointment. Tell them to disperse; and mind, don't you come back here to-night to see Dora, nor for no other reason. I'm sick myself! and I shan't see any human being except Dora this night, not even the minister. He needn't come; nobody needn't come; the door'll be locked.

Now we're alone, I'll read the letter to you, Dora, seeing you've known all about the rest of the matter, and I must tell *somebody*, or burst. Listen, and learn what confidence to repose in man:

"Dear old Girl: Don't fret yourself looking for me, as I'm seriously afraid I shall not arrive; in fact, I'm prevented by positive engagements. I drew the seven hundred dollars—all right!

much obliged. After paying up my college scrapes and settling matters around here, I find I've a cool four hundred left, with which to take a pleasure-trip to the South. In short, I'm about starting, and shall be out of hearing distance before you receive this. Don't tell anybody what a fool you've been; they might laugh at you. You were old enough to know better; but I won't reproach you.

"Ever your admiring,

"ADONIS DE MOUNTFORT."

What do you think of that, Dora Adams? "A heartless villain!" Ha! ha! You think so, do you! Well, you needn't cry, and you needn't pity me. Mehitable Green will *pity me*, I suppose. That fellow has told the truth for once in his life; I *was* too old to make such a fool of myself. I don't want pity. There! do you see that bridal-veil? I've stamped on it, and I've twisted them orange flowers into fire-kindlings. No, I ain't going to cry, and I ain't going to faint, and I ain't going to hurt myself; I'm too awful mad! Seven hundred dollars of my hard-earned savings gone, and to such a wretch! I'll kill him, if I have to follow him to the ends of the earth, I'll kill him! Seven hundred dollars, and to send me such a letter! "*Dear old girl!*" Seven hundred in good, hard money gone forever; and that isn't the worst of it—*that isn't the worst of it!* I shall be a laughing-stock to the whole of Pennyville. I shall never dare to show my face again. That Mehitable Green will be in her elements. Oh, how I hate her! how I hate the whole set! how I hate the whole world! I'll follow him; I'll track him to the other side of the earth! Seven hundred dollars, and all these wedding-clothes, and to be made a laughing-stock! He! he! boo-hoo! I've got the hysterics, I know, but I won't have 'em; I'm too mad.

Unhook this dress! tear it off of me! I can't bear the sight of it. Take it, and hang it up in the closet, and hang another one over it. And look here, Dora Adams, if ever you breathe a word about this affair, so that it gets out about my losing the money and all that, I'll never forgive you. I sent John to tell 'em Mr. de Mountfort was sick, and I mean they shall believe it. I don't know but I shall purtend he's dead, and go into mourning. I'd rather lose the other three hundred, and be thrown back on my own resources and my shop and stock in trade, than have it get to Mehitable Green's ears the way I was taken in. *That's* the worst of all; I never could stand it. I'd rather pull up stakes,

take down my sign, bar up my window, and go to some other town, and set up in business over again.

Look out, Dora, and see if the church is all

dark. Are the lights all out, and the people gone away? It's well I'm mad as I be, or I should go raving distracted; I should be in the lunatic asylum by to-morrow evening. It's just spunk that keeps me from it. There! I've kicked one of my white satin slippers into the fire. You needn't pick it out; let it burn; it does me good to see it. If I had Adonis de Mountfort in the same place, with a red-hot poker to hold him down with, wouldn't I laugh? "Dear old girl," indeed! "Old enough to know better"—ha! ha! Dora Adams, go to bed!

[The sign still creaks, with an ancient and wheezy and very doleful sound, in front of the window. We had hoped to be able to announce that the sweet face of the youthful Dora was the one which now beamed forth from that window upon the inhabitants of Pennyville; but alas! hers is still in the background, and, we are afraid, somewhat depressed by scoldings more frequent and fault-findings more severe than ever. A certain nose has grown sharper, a certain chin more peaked, a certain pair of cheeks more bloomingly red than ever, and a certain pair of eyes keep more vigilant watch out of Miss Slimmens's window. Poor woman! We have reason, from finding one of her stray poetic gems in a neglected corner, to believe that in the society of the muses she now finds her principal consolation—that, in short, she is given to

"Learn in suffering and to teach in song."

The poem we refer to seems to us to bear a faint resemblance to Hood's "Song of the Shirt;" but as the fair authoress would doubtless resent the idea, we will not mention it to the public. It is called

THE SONG OF THE HAT.

BY ALVIRA S*******

WITH ringlets many and long,
  With cheeks like roses red,
A milliner sat in her little shop,
  Plying her needle and thread.
Stitch! stitch! stitch!
  On Tuscan, Leghorn, and flat—
And still, with a voice of wonderful pitch,
  She sang the SONG OF THE HAT.

Work! work! work!
  Bleaching and trimming alone—
Work! work! work!
  For others, and not your own!

It's oh, to be a slave
  Along with the barbarous Turk,
Where part of a husband we all might have,
  If this be Christian work!

Wish! wish! wish!
  Till the brain begins to swim—
Wish! wish! wish!
  Yet never be asked by him!
Ribbon, and silk, and lace,
  Lace, and ribbon, and silk—
Yet still keep on a smiling face,
  And a look as meek as milk!

O men, with children dear!
  O widowers without wives
Forget the woman that's in her grave,
  And take the one that survives!
Bleach! bleach! bleach!
  While your darlings play in the dirt,
When I ought to be making one a frock,
  And another one a shirt!

But why do I talk of frocks,
  Or little ones playing alone?
I've looked on them with such longing eyes
  They almost seem my own—
They almost seem my own,
  Because I have not any—
Good gracious! that husbands should be so few,
  And the women who want them, so many!

Wish! wish! wish!
  And try as hard as I can!
And what do I wish for? A bed of straw,
  A crust of bread, and a man.
I've a roof and a carpeted floor,
  Tables, and dishes, and chairs—
But never a husband home to tea,
  Or a husband's step on the stairs.

Wish! wish! wish!
  Yet never to dare to speak—
Wish! wish! wish!
  From weary week to week!
Ribbon, and silk, and lace,
  Lace, and ribbon, and silk—
Yet still to keep on a smiling face,
  And a look as meek as milk!

Bleach! bleach! bleach!
  In the dull December light;
And bleach! bleach! bleach!
  When the weather is warm and bright
When all around the yard
  The clucking chickens run,
As if to show me their numerous brood,
  And twit me with having none!

Oh, but to breathe the breath
  That comes through a soft moustache!
To lean my head on a loving breast,
  Without being considered rash!

For only one short hour
  To feel as the woman feels
Who has not only a house of her own,
  But a man to come to his meals!

Oh, but for one short year
  To be some good man's wife,
Even if I were left a widow
  All the rest of my life.
A little weeping would ease my heart,
  But in their briny bed
My tears must stop, for every drop
  Is fatal to "carmine red."

With a heart that was tired to death
  Of being so old a maid,
A milliner sat in her little shop,
  Following her dreary trade.
Stitch! stitch! stitch!
  On Tuscan, Leghorn, and flat,
And still with a voice of wonderful pitch
(Would that its tones might reach some rich
Young man, it scarcely matters which),
  She sang the SONG OF THE HAT!]

THE TALLOW FAMILY

IN AMERICA.

THE

TALLOW FAMILY IN AMERICA.*

LETTER FIRST.

NIAGARA FALLS, *June*, 185—,

DEAR MIRANDA:

HERE we are at Niagara, Niagara Falls, as, may be, you have read of, as well as heard us all talk so much about when we left England. We've now been here five whole days, and seen all the sights, and many other things, of which I, may be, shall tell you some time. To-morrow,

* The reader need not be apprised that all the sayings of the family herein recorded are copiously interlarded with the aspirate, and marked by its omissions, so peculiar to a class of English people. Therefore, for American, read *Hamerican*, for hotel, read *'otel*, etc., etc.

we start for Newport, in the State of Rhode Island, I think it is. They say it is a love of a place by the sea-side—that means the ocean here —where all the sprack young men of America go every summer to keep cool by bathing all day in the surf, and by drinking cobblers at night, and waltzing and moonlight musings with the beautiful ladies. Oh, dear, *what* nice times they *must* have sitting up to their chins in water, having servants to fetch them the daily papers, and wine, and all that! I *do* wish it was *à la mode* for us Englishwomen. Don't understand me as saying that the aristocratic people here have anything to do with vulgar shoemakers. "Cobblers," is a drink these funny people make out of sherry, ice, lemon and straws. When we get there, I will write you all about it.

I wish your father hadn't been so stingy, and had let you come along with us in our travels; for (between you and me, my dear Randa) there's a good deal to be seen, though we don't let the people we meet know that we think so; else, as ma says, these Americans are *so* presumptuous they might get an idea that the English are not their superiors. You and I, my pet, don't care about such things, for we are not so wise as those as have seen much of society, like ma, since she moved up from Pud-angles to Piccadilly. It is best, I suppose, to be as haughty and grand as possible to impress them with the sense that, if we do not belong to the nobility, we've seen people as do. I am only mortified that we must be disgraced, away from home, by being classed as *commons.* It is an outrageous word, I say, and ought to be changed into something less vulgar. That would serve to give us standing away from home. Who could guess, from the way we carry our heads here, that pa is a dock chandler? Not one American. And, if we could only be rid of being classed as "commons," we should have no bounds placed to the position we could assume. But we do well, my dear. To hear ma talk, these people must all think she is a familiar in West End; that Lord Somers and Sir John Winter are her intimates; and she has, in several instances, hinted plainly that the queen's drawing-room is open to her on all state occasions. Oh, ma is true Englishwoman in carrying her head so high, I tell you, my dear! You ought to be along with us to learn how to travel.

When we arrived in New York, I thought it was Liverpool or Leeds, it was *so* big. Who would have thought these people could have such big towns? But they never can come up to London; so we shall always be above them in *that* respect. After getting off ship, our pile of luggage gave us much trouble. The "runners" was so thick just like London, for all the world; but they couldn't cry, "Carriage, sir!" "Cab, sir!" "Coach sir!" with half the lungs of the English coachee. Pa grumbled a good deal at ma's seven band and hat-boxes, nine trunks and bags, and at my own separate set. He said "he didn't know why we two women couldn't 've put our clothes together, and in two or three trunks." Oh, you ought to ha' seen how ma silenced him with a look of offended dignity! She only replied: "Mr. Tallow, show us the coach!" Had he ha' known that four of ma's trunks and two of mine were full of old clothes for effect, he *would* have blowed us.

We took coach for the Saint Nicholas Hotel, and drove up through Broadway, the most fashionable street in the country. It was much like London, though not so fine, because the houses were not so old, nor, as the French teacher used to say, so *classique*. But, I do declare, I saw things in the show-windows as fine as anything in London. This is between us, of course, for I would not tell anybody so here. I was astonished when coachee called out "Saint Nicholas!" I thought he had made some mistake, and, thinking us a noble family, had driven us to some palace, it was *so* fine. I told mother so in an under-tone; but she replied: "Hush, child! how foolish you are! There are no dukes nor lords in this country. This is a hotel for people of quality." So it was. We passed up a flight of marble steps to the second floor, where a perfect sea of rooms, and halls, and stairways, and servants, and people met our gaze. Mother walked like a queen through that assembly; but, really, nobody seemed to notice us, though I dare not tell mother so. We were ushered into a splendid suite of rooms, magnificent as the drawing-room at Windsor, as I have heard tell of; and I said to ma: "Is this where we are to sleep!" At this she showed displeasure by a slight frown; and yet I could see she was very much pleased. Indeed, she sunk down into a rich damask rolling-chair, and whispered to me: "Did you *ever*, Rosa Matilda Tallow! For all the world, it's like the Earl of Carlisle's seat, which you well remember, the steward, with whom pa had some business, allowed us to see while the family were on the Continent. Yes, indeed; it's more like great than that, for here are more big glasses, and rich hangings, and none of those smoky-looking pictures which everybody talks about as "Old Masters'.' Well, I never! But *don't you let on.*"

With this, she threw herself back in the chair, for all the world like I've heard tell of Lady Hastings, only that, as ma weighs over fifteen stone, she can't look so graceful, particularly when she is warm, and breathes loud.

"Trust Rosa Matilda Tallow *for that*," said I, resolved to begin aright, and not to impair our standing the least by being astonished at anything, nor making familiar with any one but the most elegant people. And, to show my self-reliance and ability to act my part well, I looked closely at a sweet young girl who was conversing pleasantly with an elderly gentleman on "her book." She finally observed my close attention, and turned toward me, when I lifted my eyebrows in my super-silliest manner, and, with a contemptuous look, showed her my back. I saw that ma was pleased.

Pa didn't need any lessons, evidently. He

was walking up and down the soft Turkey carpet, with a tread like an emperor, a dark frown upon his face, his lips drawn down, his arms folded, and *hauteur*, as Monsieur De Trop used to say, in his whole manner. He wanted something *better* than that, his very look showed.

A genteel-looking person came, finally, to conduct us to our rooms. He apologized for delaying us so long, saying the house was very full, and it was with difficulty the clerk could properly accommodate the Arabia's passengers. He gave us apartments on the third floor; and they were, certainly, fit for a duchess—such damask, and lace, and gilt, and mirrors, and rosewood furniture, and sweet paintings on the wall! ah! I was speechless with admiration. What was my astonishment, then, to hear ma demand loftily of the attendant "if there were no better accommodations than *this!*" He looked first surprised, and then as if he would swizzle right out in a laugh; but he didn't, and answered, humbly, there were not, "unless we wished to occupy the bridal suite of chambers, which were one hundred and fifty dollars (thirty pounds sterling) per day.

Ma almost screamed out when she heard of

such prices; but she kept her face, and replied, politely, though with a grand air still, that "these would do, she supposed, as it was their purpose to remain only long enough to see New

York two or three days at most, when they should proceed immediately to the country and the Falls."

I thought the fellow was a cunning one by the

way he looked from his eyes; but he said nothing, and left the rooms.

When the door was shut, ma fairly gave up with astonishment. "Such princely things all around really was good enough for the Princess Royal. But we must let on that it is commonplace with us," said she.

Pa moved around the rooms with dignity, his hands behind his back, after the manner of the old duke in Kensington Square, whom you remember, dear Mira, we once happened to see. He looked delighted in spite of his efforts to be serious; and I took courage to say: "Oh, so nice! Ain't you glad we've come, pa? Everybody will think we are Somervilles."

It was quite half an hour ere we could do anything but wonder and examine; and it *is* true Miranda—but don't say a word, for the world, about it—that there were things there which we never had heard of, nor knowed the use of, though ma pretended she knew all about it. But, when she took up and placed on the table what I thought *must be* a foot-cushion, and called it "an exquisite cushion for her jewels," I guessed she didn't know all about it.

We finally thought of dinner, and proceeded

to unpack. The six trunks of old clothes for effect we had stacked up in the hall, but the steward, coming along, said they must be taken in, and so pa thought, for, said he, if they should be stolen, what a tight we *should* be in! We took them in, but placed them so as to be seen every time the hall-door was opened. What to wear at dinner was now the question. It was evident, from what we had seen in the reception-rooms, that the Americans dressed richly; and, as we must outshine them, we decided upon our best—ma her purple velvet, which she had worn at the Lord Mayor's ball, to which you know we were invited because pa paid the "Times" five pounds to announce that "many of the leading residents of the Tenth have decided upon running Tudor Stuart Tallow, Esq., for alderman at the coming hustings." It was now the last of June, you know; and the purple velvet would be very warm and uncomfortable for ma; but she concluded upon it as the only thing that would "touch the right spot," as she said, meaning it would impress the people with our dignity.

I laid out a white muslin, short sleeves, low in the neck, with pink sash and pink ribbons and bow for my hair, as most becoming a very young lady, for you should know, my dear, that I intend to pass here for seventeen, if pa does insist that I look fully my age. I wore no jewels to heighten the contrast with ma, who had on the full set of "diamonds," she calls 'em; though, if these people knew anything, they would see they were no such thing.

At five o'clock, we were summoned for dinner. We were waiting, but decided to hold a little longer, that the *table d'hôte*, as you know it is called, should be well filled. Pa grumbled, for he said he was confounded hungry for a fresh chop and porter. Well, we finally started, I leaning on ma's arm, that her corpulency might set off my slender figure to the best advantage, though I dare not tell her so, for she declares she is gracefully formed. But what a disappointment awaited us! The people at this table were all dressed quite ordinary, with travelling-dresses on, shawls on their arms, and some with hats on. So busy were they eating that they did not as much as look wonderingly at us, but kept on eating and talking. Ma's face grew as red as her gown; but I carried a stiff head, I tell you, and taught her dignity. We had seats near the head of one of the tables; but it appears that there is no choice of seats here; one is just as respectable as another. Queer, ain't it?

Our servant was a real cunning-looking fellow; and I wanted to ask him his name; but I saw it wouldn't do; it might seem too familiar-like. He placed strips of paper on our plates. Ma whispered: "Now come the programmes?" I soon saw it was a list of *everything* they had to eat, and told pa he must order. He asked for chops, sandwich, and porter. "Soups first," said the servant; "mock-turtle, *à la mode*, bird's nest, alligator"— Here ma cried, "Heavens!" I saw she was frightened, and so said, "*à la mode, of course!*" with considerable emphasis. We were served, and then ordered all kinds of dishes. You ought to have seen pa eat. He took veal-pie, and roast beef, and lamb, and oyster dressing, and celery, and porter; and ma did almost the same thing when she saw that nobody noticed us.

I was seated next to a very agreeable young man, and was, of course, nice about what I eat. I was hungry, but thought it would look a little common to eat much. The young gentleman was kind to me, helped me to celery and salt, and finally entered into conversation with me in such a polite manner I knew he was a person of quality. He informed me that "everybody that was anybody was gone to the watering-places—that these people at table were on their way there, as I would perceive by their travelling habiliments—that no one stayed long in New York in the warm season, for measles were so bad." "What's that?" said ma. I whispered to her what he had said. "Heavens!" she exclaimed; "we must out of this, Tallow," but kept on eating, so that the nice young man and I had a nice time for cosseting. He said that he had spent the first five days of the watering-season, for several years, at Niagara Falls, and was now on his way there. I declare to you—in confidence, of course, my dear—that it almost made me laugh out for joy when I heard this. Oh, it would be so nice to have the society of such a man all the way there! I suppose I ought not to have admired him so much, since Lord Whipper Littleton dashed by our hired coach, one day, in Hyde Park, on his "splendid steed," as you know all the novels say. (By the way, my dear, you *must* read the novels, for it *so* enlarges your ideas, and gives you so much to talk about to educated people, like the young man I am speaking of.)

"You are *en route* for the Falls, of course," said he. "Certainly," I replied. "I shall be most happy to introduce you to the wonder of all wonders," said he. "It needs an interpreter, for its grand harmonies are overpowering to the uninitiated."

Oh! shall I confess to you, my dear Mira, how my heart throbbed at this exclamation! Who could have said this but a poet, a "living soul of fire," as you know Shelley has it? Well it was that ma was so absorbed in her dish of savories, or else she might have drawn a straight conclusion that I was "struck." Well, I listened to his conversation without reply, so completely rapt in admiration, until he asked me about the scenery of Scotland, Wales, the Hebrides, the Orkneys, and Ireland. Shame on me! I had never been to these places, and really did not know where the Orkneys were; but, *of course*, it would not do to confess my ignorance, so I replied readily to his questions, telling a straight story apparently. When he asked of the Thames and London, oh, how relieved I was! for of London you know I am *au fait*, as Monsieur De Trop used to say. When pa got that coachman in debt to him, it was a lücky day for the Tallows,

I tell you; for the fellow had to carry us around town for three whole days; and we saw everything in the city, I believe. Now, I *can* talk amazingly of London, and so can ma. My dear Mira, do try and get your pa to get some coachee in debt to him, so that you can travel over the city, for I tell you it never will do for you to go abroad, and not be able to talk like a fillip about West End, Hyde Park, Piccadilly, Parliament Row, Gravesend, Old Lion, and all.

I told the lovely young man that the Thames was the largest river in the world; that its palaces, and bridges, and barges were unequalled. He said yes, it was the original of that wonderful thing by Coleridge:

> " In Xanadu did Kubleh Khan
> A stately pleasure dome decree,
> Where Alph, the sacred river, ran
> Through bridges measureless to man,
> Down to a sunless sea."

I smiled, and said, "Oh, yes, that Coal-ridge is near the Thames, and is a wonderful thing!" Wan't that well done for me? I now talked of Brighton as the only sea-bath resort worthy of any notice in Europe. He said, "Yes; but that the Bay of Naples is pretty fair, and the Bay of

Bomarsund good, but not equal to Brighton, of course." Don't you see how he has travelled in Europe?

When ma heard the name of Brighton mentioned, she stopped eating to say, "It was at Brighton, you know, my love, Rosa Matilda, that Lord Frederick Duncy was so attentive to you. His passion for handsome curls is celebrated."

What a ma, thus to do the thing for me! Oh, I know I blushed amazingly at this! but he nearly startled my wits by saying: "Lord Frederick *has* good taste, and of course would admire your daughter's red hair." (*Red* hair! The brute! I was tempted to say. But he's evidently been in England, and knows all the nobility; so I must be pleased.) "I've no recollection of ever hearing him refer to Miss Tallow, I think," he continued. "Gracious!" exclaimed ma, dropping her silver fork, with a loud ring, upon her plate. "You don't say!" said pa; "acquainted with Lord Duncy! My boy, I'm in with you for a bottle." And here pa shoved aside his porter, ordered a bottle of sherry, and laughed out heartily. I leaned back in my chair to allow ma the pleasure of a right good look at the young gentleman. "And have you met him?" said ma. "I knew him well in London, and spent a week at his country house five years ago," he replied, quietly, as though it was nothing to spend a week at a nobleman's. "Ah!" said ma, "it is *ten* years ago that Lord Frederick was in love, or admiration, rather, with Rosa Matilda." I nearly fainted at ma's ridiculous mistake. *Ten* years ago, and I *now* only seventeen! I trod upon her toe to remind her of the blunder; but she didn't take at all, so anxious was she to escape being caught in her whopper about Lord Frederick. She groaned aloud, and exclaimed: "Heavens, my corns, Rosa!" I expected, of course, to see the young gentleman laugh right out; but he was as solemn as the Lord Chancellor, and apparently thinking of the post. He did not hear ma's exclamation, but went on to ask about Prince Albert, and the queen, and their levees. But, when we found that the young man had been in London, and associated with the nobility, we were afraid to say too much. We did not sit much longer at table, for it was becoming rather dry; so pa said, "we'd play quits." Oh, horror, Miranda! what *do* you think happened? As we arose from the table, the servant drew back our chairs; and ma, who always has to make two or three efforts before she can fairly gain her feet, had eaten so much that it was now nearly impossible for her to rise; and the careless servant, not knowing her weakness, drew away her chair at her first attempt to get up, and she sank back—heavens!—on the floor. It took pa, and Mr. Noall—which is the young man's name, we learned—and the servant, to lift her up again. She was as purple as her dress, with rage; and I was almost sick with affright and mortification. I gave up all hopes of making an impression, and saw that our first attempt had proved a failure, for certainly *now* the whole table would laugh at us; but pa here proved himself more than equal to the emergency. He tore around like one mad, and swore terribly at the servant for his carelessness, and threatened to make the house pay dearly for such an outrage upon persons of quality. This appeared to give us much consideration, for all the table stopped eating, and noticed us particularly as we passed out, ma on the arm of pa, and I—shall I say it?—on the arm of Mr. Noall, who seemed all attention.

We kept our room after that, for ma was

lame; and pa said he could drink his porter and eat his cheese with more peace than at table. I did not like this proceeding, but made free to go down to the parlors, where I met Mr. Noall several times, and "formed his permanent acquaintance," as he confessed. Oh, how I do thrill all over at the thought of him! Just to think that that grease-weigher of pa's ever should think of *my* hand!

After remaining at the Saint Nicholas for nearly three days, we started for Albany, I think it is called, on the Hudson River. Oh, what a fairy boat! It was named after our great Sir Isaac Newton, who discovered the apple falling from the tree, and thereby explained the reason of the world's being hung on its centre at Greenwich Hospital, as you've heard it is. Such fixings I never dreamed of, nor read of. It was all gold, and silver, and lace, and Turkey carpets, and mirrors. It *is* astonishing how these Americans do things. I declare I don't know if the queen dreams of the way these people are going ahead! When I get home, I shall try and gain admittance to her just to warn her of the true state of things here. She must know it, or England will've much to "hang her harp on the willow-trees" for. There! ain't that well said for a humble woman?

How do you think I felt, dear Mira, in the midst of such splendor, and Mr. Noall on the same boat? My emotions were as tumultuous as one of the kettles in pa's factory. I saw myself reflected all around me; and it recalled Mr. Moore's Lally Rook's palace. I only wanted Mr. Noall's arm round me to be transported to Peri. I know the crowd of elegant passengers must've read something inspiring in my face, for they looked wonderingly at me. Ma had to call me several times before I could come back to myself, and go and prepare for a promenade on deck. Ma "well knew Mr. Noall would come and ask me to walk," she said. Has she guessed my secret? I asked my heart. It said, in loud tones, "No!" I dressed in my rose-colored, heavy flounced *barège* with pink sash, and cameo pin in my bosom. Thus dressed, I stepped into the cabin, and really surprised all the ladies there. They were dressed quite common, in linen travelling-dresses and very common bonnets. Soon Mr. Noall came along. As he did so, he bowed rather coldly to a young lady, who, I declare, was the same young woman I looked at so super-silly in the parlor of the Saint Nicholas. How glad I was that I had so noticed her! for it was plain she wa'n't much from the way Mr. Noall recognized her. She was dressed in the same linen travelling-dress she had on then. How vulgar! He came along, and, bowing very low to me, said "he hoped I was gay as a blackbird in a crow's nest."

"As a nightingale, you mean," I said.

"Oh, yes, I forgot—a nightingale in England, and the blackbird in America," he said. "Will you not flutter on deck, awhile, this transcendent morning?" "Certainly," I said; and forthwith we went out upon deck. Oh, such delicious conversation as we had! It now all comes back to me like a thing that hasn't happened, because it is too good to be true.

Almost before I was aware, we were in sight of Albany. I then had to resume my travelling suit, for we were to take the first train to the Falls. All the passengers lunched on the boat; but I was too happy for eating.

At Albany, I lost sight of Mr. Noall. We knew he was to stop at the International Hotel, for he said it was there the beauty and Creoles gathered. Creoles means a young lady with some aboriginal blood of Indian and French in 'em, you should know. So we resolved to go there. Ma was better of her lameness, and talked of her first appearance at an American watering-place with a good deal of humor. She said she meant to dress in short clothes to clamber around at the Falls. But pa said: "No you don't with me. Long clothes and dignity, short clothes and street gals," he said, with a queer wink of the eye. So ma said, as she expected to stick to him like a piece of tallow, she must stick to long skirts, she supposed. With such rich sallies of humor did we while along the time. I was rather quiet, from thinking not only of Mr. Noall, but of the Creoles and of what I was to wear. I scarcely thought of the Falls.

"Here we are at the Falls at last," said pa. "I hope we shall find the real Barclay here, not that villainous hock ale we had to guzzle at Albany." "And I hope," said ma, "that we shall have for dinner a brace of swans and a musk ox, for I am *so* fond of wild game." I only hoped Mr. Noall would be there; that was all, though I durst not say it.

"Marcy me! hear it thunder!" exclaimed ma, as we took seats in the 'bus. "Where *is* our baggage? Oh, coachee, run and get our trunks —seventeen of 'em; that's all—and six band-boxes and bags," said ma to the 'bus man. "Your gentleman has taken his checks and gone for the baggage, ma'am," said the man. "Yes, but hurry him; it's going to rain," cried ma. "Rain? not a bit of it," said the man. "Why, it's thundering terribly!" "Oh, that's the Falls roaring!" said coachee; and sure enough it was. But I was perfectly unconcerned; something else filled my bosom than the Falls. "What was it?" you say. Why, it was the Creoles, and Mr. Noall, and my first appearance, of course.

Just then, pa came rushing up to the 'bus, and, sticking his head in, said: "Oh, Mrs. Tallow, we are ruined! Two of those big black trunks is broken down, and robbed—nothing left in them but some candle-boxes with my card on 'em. All the valuable contents gone!" Ma did not move, nor appear excited. "Why don't you say something. *Mrs.* Tallow?" cried pa. "Mr. Tallow," said ma, "don't give yourself any more trouble. If those old trunks have broken down, it is no loss." "No loss? You are crazy! I tell you your clothes are all gone, and nothing left but some candle-boxes and old bagging," said pa. "*Just what I put in 'em,*" said ma. "Now, don't make a fool of yourself, Mr. Tallow, but get in here, and let the old trunks go," put in ma. Pa only said "Humph!" and seemed to be struck with an idea, for he soon roared with laughter, crying: "Oh, you are one of 'em, Mrs. Tallow! one of 'em, I say! You'll do to travel; you will. Old England against the milliners!" With that, we started for the hotel.

The International is not so big nor so fine as the Saint Nicholas. The rooms are smaller, less genteelly furnished, and up in the fourth story—at least, there was where we were placed. Pa got mad about the meanness of the rooms—nothing but ingrain carpet on the floor, cottage beds, lace curtains, and sofas, and chairs, and one large mirror. Pa said he wouldn't stand *that.* The clerk replied: "That or nothing!" when pa called him up; and so we had to put up with it.

After dressing, ma and me took to the halls, which were very long, and wide, and cool. Ma was dressed in her black satin, bought, you know, at the sale of Mrs. Snuffy's effects. I had on my *barège*, only with blue trimming in my hair, and no sash on. We cut quite a stiff, I tell you; but we found some women whose dresses were rich enough for queens. Where the Creoles were, we could not tell; probably on the other floors; so down we went to see. Whom should we meet but Mr. Noall, in company with several other young men, gaily enjoying the time?

"Why, Miss Rosa Matilda Tallow! I declare! And Mrs. Lolly Jane Tallow! How do you do?" And he shook hands with us so heartily, it tore my glove, and actually started the bodice of ma's dress. "Glad to see you, to converse with you, to promenade with you. Allow me the exquisite pleasure of your arms." So saying, he offered his elbows; and, with ma on one side, and your gay Rosa Matilda on the other, he started down the long hall with so proud an air, it did my very soul good to admire him I was delighted, of course, and so was ma, for she swelled out amazingly, and swung herself in real West End style. Oh, the nice things he said, poet that he is! I gave away my heart to him entirely, and could only look in his face, and smile.

"Have you seen the Falls yet?" said he, suddenly. I really had not thought of them, and so with ma. We were too absorbed upon our first appearance; but we dare not confess *that*, for it would be provoking to an American to see that people like us should think so little of the Great Cataract. So I replied that I only awaited pa to escort us out. "Allow me the pleasure of your company, Miss Tallow. Mr. Tallow must be satisfied with the company of his adorable lady," he said, with a low bow and sweet smile. Ma was too well-bred to refuse this offer for my society; and so off we started for Mr. Tallow. We found him looking after us. He said "he had found some real Barclay down below, and now was braced for a drive at the Falls." I hurried before ma, put on my jaunt hat, which, you know, was taken from our Lancashire girl for tearing ma's old gingham dress in washing it. I looked charming, I assure you, my love. My *barège* took an air of grace from the hat and its long ribbons; and I felt so elated that I know I must have been very youthful appearing. So Mr. Noall thought, for he said: "Miss Rosa

Matilda, you look so much more charming to-day than I ever saw you before, that I wondered at your modesty in excluding yourself so much. Lord Frederick ought to see you now." I could have thrown my arms round him for this speech. I only wish ma could've heard it. I could only say: "It is flattering to be so appreciated by a person of your quality, and only trust I shall become more charming in your eyes," looking him full in the face. He colored beautifully at this, and said, fervently: "Impossible! impossible!"

By this time we arrived at the observatory, I think it is; but, instead of going up, Mr. Noall took me out on a long platform, projecting over the high bank. I was really horror-struck at the dangerous place, and had to shrink back; but he said: "Faint heart never won brave man;" so I slowly followed out to the end of the platform.

My eyes! There was the Falls in all their majestic magnitude before us. I was dumb-founded for more than a minute. I had thought of something like the Caermarthen Cascades, which Uncle Dawylin took me to when I was a child, in Wales; but la! these were so much bigger, I could not take them all in at once.

"What do you think of them?" said Mr. Noall. "Oh, beautiful! adorable! very fine!" said I. "Anything like them in England?" said he. "Well, really, I can't say. Caermarthen Cascades are not so great," said I. "Do you think the queen would admire them?" said he. "I should think so," said I. "I shall tell her of them at my interview, when I go home." "You going to have an interview with Victoria?" said he. Then I saw what a goose I had made of myself. Could I tell him the object of that interview, and thus betray my country? Never! So I said: "Yes, sir; I hope to see the queen, when I return to England, to relate to her all that I've seen. I may give her some hints which she would like." Wa'n't that diplomatically done? "Give my love to her," was his reply. "Lord! is *he* in love with the queen?" I said to myself. Oh, the agony of that moment! I said immediately: "Let us return, Mr. Noall, for I feel unwell." "Dizzy," said he, "from too much elevation of person."

So we wended our way back to the hotel. I was quite silent; but he rattled on like the carriage wheel of a duke. After a while, he left me, "to rest after the long walk," he said, and promised to see me on the morrow, and take me all around the place. I withdrew to my room to ruminate on the infidelity of man and the fickleness of love.

Pa and ma did not come in till dark. They had hired a coach, and made the fellow drive as long as he could see. They talked, and talked, and wondered, and drank a bottle of Barclay, and asked me all kinds of questions, until I told them to leave me to my musings; when ma said, "I was growing poetical with that Mr. Noall," and left me to myself. Pa was, and has been, ever since our arrival, on his high heels, as the American boys express exuberant fun; and so has ma. She laughs and talks to every well-dressed person, and makes herself generally agreeable, for all her notions about being exclusive. But, it is true, everybody here is really aristocratic. So we don't want to throw ourselves on our dignity much.

And I, do you say, dear? I am really head and ears in love with Mr. Noall. He is so charming! so devoted! so complimentary! It would take a volume to tell all the good things he has said. He danced with me, last night, at the general reception ball; and I tell you he did it like a count. Oh, I am so delighted here, and wish I could stay; but pa says "No!" And so to-morrow we are off for Newport. Mr. Noall says he will be there too, in a few days; so I am not disconsolable.

Oh, to be loved! I say all the time!

Adieu, my dear, until I write from Newport.

No more. My heart, be still.

For the present,

ROSA MATILDA TALLOW.

LETTER SECOND.

NEWPORT, *July*, 185-.

DEAR MIRANDA:

I IMPROVE the first opportunity, since our arrival at this sweet place, to continue informing you of what happens to me in this country, as I promised. This, Mr. Noall says, is the Brighton of America. I am writing to you, my love, within the sound of ocean's roar—or would be, if there was not so much noise to prevent.

This morning I had a charming walk on the beach with Mr. Noall. He appears to be a very sentimental young man. Every glance of his sweet, dark eyes inspired me to say something romantic.

"Are you fond of the sea?" said I. "Very," said he; "more than you would believe." "Ah!" said I, "a scene like this always reminds me of those beautiful verses of Tom Moore's:

"'Roll on, thou deep and dark blue ocean! roll!'

He describes my emotions so naturally when he says:

"'The scattered waters rave,
And the winds their revels keep;'

doesn't he yours, Mr. Noall?" "Then you enjoyed the voyage across?" said he. "Intensely," said I; "the sailors were so picturesque in their blue jackets, and the ocean was so sublime."

(The truth is, dear, I was so horribly sea-sick all the way, that I was only out on deck once; and I thought then the seamen were nasty creatures, and the ocean was nothing to brag of, giving one such an uncomfortable sensation, and taking away all one's appetite for the turtle-soup which the captain handed me with his own hands at dinner.)

But I must go back to the beginning, that you may understand how Mr. Noall and I came to be walking on the beach at Newport together. Well, I made it a point to have pa leave Niagara in the same train with him. I was provoked almost beyond endurance, you'd better believe, when I saw, in the same car with us, the young lady I have before mentioned. Her father, I suppose it is, was with her. They came in after us, and took seats in front of us, not very far away. She seemed to me to be a little paler than before; and I fancied a sad look about her mouth, which, I must say, I was not sorry to see, if Mr. Noall had anything to do with her being so melancholy. I was looking right at her when he came in from seeing to his baggage; and she flushed up as pink as my paint-saucer, and then got whiter than ever; he just bowed to her without speaking, said something about the weather to her father, and then came and sat down by me, asking my permission in the most elegant manner. Of course, I was only too glad to give it. He sat by me all the way to Buffalo, talking so gay, and making himself so agreeable to pa and ma, and was so attentive about the draught coming in the windows, and about my shawl, that I began to be certain he meant something particular. I was in the seventh heaven of happiness; and all the time the young lady, whom I heard her father call Emmeline, got stiller and sadder. At first, she tried to be merry, and make her pa smile; but, at last, she just turned and looked out of the window; and he read his paper in quiet.

At Buffalo—a big town, where Mr. Noall informed me the buffaloes came to drink out of Lake Erie before the place was settled—my hapness was brought to a sudden termination. The young man arose, and wished us good-day, saying he was going no further at present. I presume I looked disappointed, for he said, with one of his smiles that make me feel so flustrated: "But I hope to meet you at Newport, Miss Tallow, before you have been there a week." So I had nothing to do but anticipate; and I should have been quite certain of his intentions if the girl and her pa had not also parted company with us at the same time.

I do think ma knows about as well as the best how to play her cards. I assure you she did not let the opportunity slip for deepening the favorable impression which my arts were making upon the young man who had once spent a week with My Lord Frederick Duncy.

"I feel some compunctions, Mr. Noall," she told him, as we rode along—this was before he left us, of course—"in taking our Rosa Matilda to an American watering-place. They say that everybody goes to such places in this country, and Rosa has always been so select in her company. Things are *so* different in London, you know, where people are not obliged to come in contest (contact, she meant) with the vulgar, Mr. Noall. And she is so young and inexperienced. Of course, she'll be sought after; for a girl with twenty thousand pounds on her wedding day, is not to be slighted. But how to tell the high from the low here, is what I want to know. I hope we shall not be imposed upon. We shall expect you to be a protector to Rosa Matilda;

she is so unsuspicious." "I trust her innocence will be her best shield," was his sweet reply. "My twenty thousand pounds, made by hard earnings in the candle business"—(I nearly screamed out here, Miranda, pa's such a fool about such things)—"shan't go to any low-bred American," growled pa. "He's got at least to have been in old England, and associated with the aristocracy, whoever he is, before he gets the first penny of it." "Mr. Noall knows 'em all," said ma.

It was just here that the train stopped, and we lost him.

"I guess your twenty thousand pounds made him stare," remarked ma, after we were on our way again. "I hope, Rosa Matilda, that you will take advantage of the present favorable opportunities. It is true that *no* American can be a person of title; but, if the nobility chooses to associate with this young man, I don't see why we should hold *our* heads any higher. I hope your arts will be more successful than they were at Brighton." "If 'practice makes perfect,' Rosa ought to be perfect by this time," said pa, who, you know, has not got the temper of an angel. "I almost think you're a born idiot, at times, Mr. Tallow," cried ma. "What in the name of sense do you speak about the candle business for, just at that inauspicious moment when I was plotting for my daughter's welfare? Do you think I can see her prospects of happiness thus ruthlessly overthrown by her own flesh-and-blood relative, her father, and sit still in my seat?" She was obliged to sit still in her seat, for, I assure you, her size did not admit of much fidgeting about in a railroad-carriage seat. "Do be a little more circumspectuous after this, Mr. Tallow!" "It's my opinion a soap-and-candle factory ain't any too strong for American noses," replied pa, in a huff. "For Heaven's sake, pa, do speak a little lower!" said I. "When we might just as well pass for people who inherited their money, what's the use in letting it be known you made it? Now, you know, with that grand air of yours, you might as well pass for the Lord Mayor himself, or perhaps a baronet, if you'd be quiet about the chandler's shop."

I know better how to manage him than ma. The idea of being mistaken for a baronet put him in a good humor at once; and he has not mentioned the shop since. On the contrary, he orders the servants about grander than ever;

and I cannot tell you how pleased I was to find that he had entered our names on the book at the Ocean House as "*Sir* Tudor Stewart Tallow, wife, and daughter."

Oh, Miranda, I wish my pen could do justice to my emotions, and give you a faint idea of what a love of a place this is! But the charges are ruinous; and I don't believe pa would stay a week, if ma did not persuade him that a few days' expense might bring about an engagement between me and Mr. Noall. And, indeed, I think so myself, he's so extremely polite to us; and the very thought keeps me in such a flutter that I am actually losing my appetite.

We had a choice of rooms upon arriving here, for it's too early in July for the "season" to be fairly commenced. There's not much of a jam yet, though the hotels are full. Ma wanted to take a "sweet" of rooms with a parlor that was offered to us; but the price was so enormous that pa flatly refused. We have two bedrooms; and I tell ma, when I want to vex her, that we will have to order the partition between them taken down to give her a chance to turn round. If it was not for the ocean breezes, we would suffocate in the act of dressing; and that's the most of the time here; for the ladies of this country beat my eyes with their beautiful clothes. I never saw anything like it—so superb! I tell you we can't begin to shine, and could not more than equal them if all our trunks full of old clothes were crowded with elegant things from Paris. But mother's paste diamonds are so sumptuous that she does not need so much variety. As for me, I affect the simplicity of seventeen; while pa gives people very plainly to understand that it is not because Rosa Matilda has not the guineas at her fingers' ends that she does not have as many dresses as Queen Victoria.

Oh, Miranda, such dancing and waltzing as we have here every night is enough to bewilder one with ecstasy! The young men are, all of them, delightful; though I have seen none, as yet, the superior of Mr. Noall, except that I admire the manners of some more—they are so dashing, and say such funny things. However, my heart is given to the first-mentioned; and I shall never love another. I feel it through every fibre of my existence!

Speaking of him reminds me again to begin at the beginning. Yesterday being our third day here, I was looking out the window at the arrival of the omnibus, when I saw him get out. How my heart palpitated, as he sprang so elegantly to the ground! And how overjoyed I was to see that the young lady who had excited my jealousy was not with him! I finished dressing for dinner, and went down in the parlor in the hopes of a meeting with him immediately. Wishing to appear pensive in his absence, I sat down to the piano, and sang, in my most impassioned style, "'Tis said that absence conquers love." As I was dwelling upon the last line, I was conscious of his entrance into the room, though I did not cast my eyes that way, but fixed them upon the ceiling. There was an admiring crowd around the instrument, listening to my music. As I ceased, I allowed my gaze to descend from the ceiling, until my eyes met his; *then* I gave a little start of surprise, and immediately left the instrument, as if overcome. *He* was not the only one affected by my little bit of acting. As I crossed the apartment, I heard a splendid-looking young man murmur under his breath: "Heavens! what emotion must not such youth, beauty, and constancy inspire in the breast of him who awakes it!" "United with such golden ringlets and other golden charms," whispered another gay fellow by his side.

"So you arrived in safety, Miss Tallow. How are your parents? I trust you have been enjoying yourself," said Mr. Noall, coming and sitting by me as soon as I reached a sofa. "I have been living upon hope," replied I, archly. "Ah!" said he; "that is unsubstantial food. Perhaps that is the reason you so much resemble an ethereal being, Miss Tallow. You are so light and airy, one almost looks to see you flutter away in a cloud of your own pink ribbons."

I blushed and smiled, inwardly resolving to eat no more roast beef, even to deny myself plum-pudding and ale, if necessary to keep up my delicate appearance. Ma says I am too thin; and pa says I am scrawny; but I think Mr. Noall's taste is as good as theirs.

That evening, I wore my handsomest ball-dress, and had Monsieur Frizzle to curl my hair. My dress was of sky-blue satin, trimmed with primroses, with an Indian gauze scarf twisted in the back of my hair, and floating down my shoulders. I flatter myself the scarf gave me the appearance of an angel with wings as I moved in the dance. Mr. Noall asked me to dance the mazurka, and had just led me to a seat when I saw, standing inside the door, as if they had just entered the ball-room, the young girl and her father. I have learned their names from Mr. Noall, for I asked him straight out who they were. Mr. Stanley, the father, is an ex-senator of the United States, and a distinguished politician. His daughter, Emmeline, is his only child; and he takes her everywhere with him. They are very aristocratic, I should judge, from the attentions paid them. Mr. Noall likewise told me they resided in the same city with himself. I cannot deny to you that she is beautiful. She has large bright eyes of the softest brown, an oval face with *real* color in her cheeks—just the faintest, except when she blushes—and the loveliest hands and arms, and the glossiest hair. Her dress was not so low in the neck as the most; and she wore a jacket of exquisite lace that must have cost a sum of money, and come up around her white throat, and fastened with a pearl brooch. Of course, she is a prude! How I do hate 'em, the affected things!

When Mr. Noall told me who they were, I was anxious to become acquainted with them, and hinted as much, but he did not offer to introduce me. I noticed that she received a great deal of attention; but need I attempt to express how glad I felt when I saw that Mr. Noall did not offer to dance with her at all, nor even speak to her, but danced with me twice, and asked me, when we parted in the ball-room, to walk on the beach with him the next morning?

And so it happened that I was so supremely fortunate as to promenade with him by the "shore of the surging sea." We walked along the beach where the ladies, and children, and their gentleman attendants, were bathing in the surf. It was a very animated scene. As my companion said, "it reminded him of the possibility of mermaids, combing their golden tresses with their fingers." And he looked at my ringlets, as much as to say I would make a pretty mermaid. I thought I would myself, and was hoping he would ask me to go in the water, although I had some doubts about its being entirely modest to go in with any one except one's father or relative.

As we stood on the beach, who should hurry past us, while we were looking at some children frolicking in the waves, but Mr. Stanley and his daughter, on their way to the bath-houses, a few steps off, to change their bathing-dresses. They did not see who we were. They had been in the surf, and the young lady's cheeks were as red as roses; and her hair had come down, and the wet had made it part into a thousand little shining curls; and her little bare feet were as delicate as sea-shells. I saw Mr. Noall's eyes following her until she disappeared. I thought the full Turkish trowsers, and all that, were very romantic; and I secretly longed to see myself attired in them, and feel the delicious sensation of the sea breaking over me in the arms of Mr. Noall. But I shall have to wait until we are married (oh, Miranda, how that sounds!) for I've discretion enough to know that the water would wash every trace of the rose-pink from my cheeks, and that, instead of making my hair curl like Miss Stanley's, it would straighten it out into anything but beautiful locks; and, as for my feet, dear, *you* know, confidentially, that they never were as plump as pin-cushions, nor as soft as lily-leaves.

Well, there we stood for full ten minutes; and, upon my word, Mr. Noall never took his eyes off the little cabin in which the young lady had disappeared!

"You seem to be indulging in a very abstracted meditation," I remarked, at last, with just enough meaning in my tone to convey to him that I was aware of where his thoughts were roving. "Ah, Miss Tallow, there is a charm in this vicinity—the ocean, you know, and—the—the"— And here he broke right off, and stared at Miss Stanley, who had emerged from the bath-house in the sweetest morning-dress, and such a cunning little hat on, and her hair tucked up under it, and half of it blowing about her face in a way to awaken jealousy in the most angelic breast. Her father was waiting for her, and gave her his arm. As they passed, he spoke: "Ha! good-morning, Edward!" as if he had been addressing a very intimate friend: but the girl only bowed; and I was positive I saw a slight smile come over her face as she glanced at me. I expected her to frown with envy; but she didn't; but, after they were gone by, and I looked up at my companion, *he* was frowning and biting his lips. After that, he was not near so communicative as before; and we were having rather a silent time of it back to the hotel. When we arrived, and went on to the piazza, Miss Stanley was there, with a book; and Mr. Noall commenced making himself ten times more agreeable than ever. As we walked past her so close that she must have heard, he said, in his sweetest manner: "May I consider you engaged to ride with me this afternoon at six?" "With mamma's consent, I shall be too happy," I replied; and I was afraid he could see how my heart fluttered at this unexpected honor.

So, as pa and ma were standing by the railing, conversing with two or three dashing-looking people, we approached them.

"Ah, here comes my darling Rosa!" exclaimed ma, in the warmest manner, as she perceived us. "I hope the bathing was not too much for your nerves, my child, and that Mr. Noall has taken good care of you. But of course he has done that," she continued, smiling at him as if he were already her son, and tapping his shoulder with her fan. Pa was busy talking with the gentlemen. He wore his red velvet vest; and I thought he was looking very well. "For foreigners are rather hard upon us," one of the gentlemen, a very quiet-looking person, was saying. "Dickens, for instance, repaid our admiration rather roughly." "Dickens's career in this country, sir," replied pa, in his grandest style, and unbuttoning his waistcoat to throw out his chest, "was a warning to me. I almost resolved to travel among the Americans, incognito, to avoid the troublesome attentions which befell him. 'It will never do,' I said to myself, 'to write myself down Sir Tudor Stewart Tallow, in that country, if I would be safe from the populace.' But Lady Tallow did not agree with me upon the propriety of placing ourselves upon an equality with the 'vulgar throng,' as she very properly expressed herself; and so we ventured upon retaining the family title." "I hope your health has not suffered from extreme persecutions of the kind your great novelist was subjected to," said the gentleman, with a polite smile.

What more they said, I did not stop to hear, for I was so flustrated with Mr. Noall's offer, that I wanted to fly to my apartment to think it over, and communicate my hopes to ma, who followed me up-stairs to learn if anything had happened particular during our walk. "I consider it as good as a proposal of marriage," said ma, decidedly. And so do I, dear; and you may imagine the state of anticipation I am in. It's a wonder I can write at all. In one hour,

Miranda, it will be the appointed time for that ride which is to decide my destiny. I can hardly hold my pen to say more; and I have, besides, to go and put on that sweet orange silk of mine for the drive.

One thing is certain. Mr. Noall means to give that young lady to understand that Americans cannot hope to shine when there are foreign stars around. His manner toward her has said as much. I am so glad we came. Pa grumbles at the expense; but, when he gets me so well off his hands, I think he will be satisfied. The adoption of his title keeps him in pretty good humor, too. But, positively, no more until to-morrow, or until I can write you particulars of the happy news, which I shall do as soon after as I am sufficiently composed. In a tumult of blissful sensation,

Your fortunate

ROSA MATILDA TALLOW.

LETTER THIRD.

NEWPORT, *July*, 185–.

MY DEAR MIRANDA:

IT was in a flood of gorgeous anticipations that I closed my last. My happiness is not yet complete; but I am in a state of hope which I have not been in since you and I were at Brighton. America is indeed a sweet place. I care not what pa nor the British Parliament says about it; it's a dear, sweet place, especially for young ladies. My only wish, Miranda, is that you were here; that is my only wish, except the one which I feel is soon to be gratified. Pa talks a good deal with the gentlemen about the dismissal of our minister, and says he wonders the English nation did not declare war against the United States at once; but, despite of all that, he grows better-natured every day, and does not growl half so much as usual when ma and I ask him for a little pin-money. The reason of his good temper is that all the visitors here have got to calling him Sir Tudor, when they address him, and ma, Lady Tallow. You can't imagine what an effect this has upon pa—and ma, too, as for that matter. I am sometimes afraid that his accent will betray him, for you remember how all my frettings never could induce him to drop that horrid habit of misplacing all his h's. Still, as everybody calls him Sir Tudor, and treats him with the greatest attention, I presume we pass for the real thing. I've seen some of the young ladies tittering, sometimes, when they were saying things to him, and ma, and I, which we did not exactly understand; and, though they sounded like very polite things, I have sometimes suspected they were poking fun at us. Young ladies, especially those pert creatures who ought still to be in their pinafores, can be *so* disagreeable when they choose, especially when the spiteful things are envious; and I can see that the attentions of Herbert Noall (Herbert! isn't *that* a sweet name, darling?) is half killing them with envy of me. Speaking of pa and the minister reminds me of another little fear I have, which is almost the only cloud upon the heaven of my summer's enjoyment; and that is that there is talk of Lord Napier's being in Newport; and some of the company are looking for him every train that arrives. If he should come before I have secured Mr. Noall, I don't know what the consequences will be; for we have pretended to such an intimacy with the nobility, that everybody will expect us to know him well, and to present them to him. Indeed, they are all talking to us about him now, and asking all sorts of questions; so that I believe ma tells more fibs every day on his account than her conscience will ever forgive her for. Pa can tell stories without so much danger of tripping, for he has often seen him in public places in London; but ma nor I never laid eyes on him in our lives. Ma came pretty near getting into a scrape yesterday. Somebody got her to describe Lord Napier's personal appearance and manners, and then coolly told her that pa had just represented him very different. I felt the color spreading over my face and neck, for I did not see what ma could do; but she said, very quietly, that Sir Tudor was always confounding Lord Napier with Sir Lytton, with both of whom he was very intimate; and he must have been speaking with his usual absent-mindedness. Oh, dear! I do hope he will stay away, at least a few days longer. How unfortunate it would be to have that lord arriving here just in time to ruin the hopes which I have erected for the hundredth time, and this time the brightest of all!

When I closed my last, it was to take that eventful ride with Mr. Noall. Well, I dressed in my best, and rode down along the beach by his side. The evening was lovely, and the road was crowded; and I, your Rosa Tallow, had the handsomest beau; and he had the finest turn-out there was upon the beach. My heart was in my mouth the most of the time, for I was sure that he was upon the verge of a proposal. I saw it in his eyes—not that I ever had a genuine proposal, or can speak from experience (between you and I, pet), but just as it is described in novels. He sighed several times; and his manner was so obstructed that I was sure we should run into somebody's vehicle, or they would into ours; and I nearly screamed at the danger of upsetting at least three times. The ride came to an end, as all earthly bliss must; and he had not committed himself, except by his actions. "They spoke louder than words."

When we arrived in front of our hotel, I saw

the pale face of Miss Stanley glance from behind a curtain, and instantly withdrew. I thought there were tears in her large eyes; and I am sure she grows thinner and quieter every day. Mr. Noall saw her too. He had not spoken for the last ten minutes; but he handed me out of the carriage with *such* a bow as was eloquence itself. Ma was waiting in the parlors, looking out for me, and hurried me to my room to ask if the matter was settled. I was obliged to confess that it was not; but, when I told of my companion's manner, she was satisfied, and so was pa, and so pleased with that, and with the respect paid him down-stairs, that he voluntarily, for the first time in his life, pulled out his wallet, and gave me enough money to send to New York, and order a new ball-dress for the grand first ball of the season, which comes off to-morrow at this hotel. I have sent my orders, along with several other ladies, and expect a perfect love of a dress to arrive in a bandbox to-morrow morning. In the meantime, I am to have another ride. Just think of it! This afternoon, I go out again with Mr. Noall; and he has not taken another unmarried lady out since he came, not even Miss Stanley, who just bows to him now.

'Tis evening, now; and I am another woman, a poor, broken-hearted creature; and, while I write, ma is in a fit of dumps too deep to say anything; and pa strides up and down the room, muttering great oaths about these Americans, these wretches that they are. I will tell you how it all happened. It is a dreadful tale.

In the afternoon, at three, Noall—the brute! the beast! the animal that he is!—drove up; and, all expectancy, I descended from the piazza to the carriage. Off we drove, in fine style, I assure you, for it was a splendid establishment, such as I never dreamed of riding with. We went into the interior, where nature was most wooing, for there, I thought, surely he must propose. On the way, whom should we pass but Miss Stanley—the mean, deceitful wretch!—and her pa, who were driving out in their own establishment, which had just come on that day. They passed us quickly, and only gave Noall—the wretch!—a cold bow, as usual. His cheek, I saw, turned first red as beer, then pale as tallow; but he was very devoted to me, and leaned over his head so near as actually to touch my shoulder. What a delicious sensation it *did* produce! I only wish you, my dear thing, could realize the "magic of that touch," as the poetic grinder used to sing by our back door. Oh, the wretch, to thus dare to touch my feelings! Well, I was in too much ecstasy of bliss to note anything, and hardly knew that he had turned his horse's head toward the beach. We were soon on the thronged highway, where there is always such a funny sight—the ocean, the people in all manner of dresses, some for a walk, some on horseback, some in carriage, some going and some coming from the bathing-rooms, and some up for all manner of things. *Here* my tragedy of life is written. Oh, would I had never been born! or, at least, would that I had never seen Newport! Wretched place! How can I tell you what happened? But I will, just to ease my heart, which feels like a tallow barrel with the hoops all bursted off, to use the expressive words of pa.

We came down to the beach-road in fine style. My blue ribbons streamed out grandly. I sat up, looking like the queen, I know, so full of pride and dignity did my bosom feel. I scorned the vulgar people around me; and I could see, as we passed, how they envied us. Oh, I can't go on! but I *must*. I will out on him, the wretch!

We were going along down the beach rapidly, when we saw a carriage coming toward us like the wind. People screamed, and rushed away, some into the surf, and some into the gardens. I saw, with my eaglet's eye, that it was a furious runaway. "Oh, Mr. Noall, drive away; anywhere, I say!" I screamed. But he stopped his team dead still, as true as I live, the brute! On the carriage came; and, when it neared us, I saw—oh dear!—that it was Mr. Stanley's carriage, and that the driver was thrown from his seat, and the lines on the ground. One line caught in the wheel, and turned the horses' heads right in the water; and, as true as cattle-day, they plunged right into the surf. It was done all in a moment. A long shriek came from the carriage; and then all on shore held their breath in silence. But, quick as thought, Noall sprang from my side, gave the lines to a gardener standing near, and then plunged into the surf after the carriage. I would have swooned, but confess that I was mad and mortified that he should leave me to rescue Miss Stanley—the vixen!—from drowning. I sat almost stupefied. He swam after the horses, now several rods out in the sea, and plunging terribly.

In a minute, as it were, he was at the carriage—he sprang upon the driver's seat—he pulled out first the old man, Stanley, and then Miss Stanley; and, placing his arms around the creature—oh that she had drowned!—he leaped into the water, and soon brought her to shore. The old man soon followed in the arms of two other men, who, by this time, had the courage to go to the rescue.

What do you think were my feelings all *this* time? But what will you think when I tell you Noall stooped over the body of Miss Stanley, and pressed his lips to hers, and placed her hands in his bosom, while he actually raised her head in his arms? Oh, my agony was indescribable! But there is no end to some people's misery (pa says, no more than there is to a fall in the market when tallow gets to going down), for the wretch actually brought her to our own carriage; he placed her in it; and, while she reclined upon his breast, he drove rapidly to the hotel. The old man followed in another carriage. I assure you I looked at that base man at my side with a power that would have melted stone; but he did not appear to notice me at all; his whole soul seemed to be bound up in that swooning woman in his arms. I resolved to have an explanation of *such* conduct, and bore with it in silence.

When we reached the hotel, he himself carried her up to her room, and gave her in charge of a physician, never thinking of me, whom he actually left sitting in the carriage. Pa came up, and took me out, and asked: "Are you frightened, my posey?" "No," said I indignantly; "I am an outraged woman!" For, indeed, I was so in many ways. Not only had my feelings been injured, but, I declare, my pink lawn was completely ruined by that woman's wet clothes, my head-dress was all dishevelled and smashed, and all my perfumes and rich roses were gone. I looked no more like Rosa Matilda Tallow, the envied beauty of the morning, than the willow looks like the oak. "I am an outraged woman!" I cried again; and don't you think the *gentlemen* standing around actually laughed out, instead of coming forward, as I expected them to do, to resent my injured honor. What a story it is to call these Americans "brave men," "chivalrous to women!" They don't understand what belongs to such virtue and dignity as they know we possess. Pa saw how it was, and took me to my room, muttering: "Outrageous! He shall pay for the dress, and account to me for all other damage." It wasn't *that* I cared for, but my injured position. But, dear man, he didn't seem to see things in the same light. He was a little "tight," as I think Noall calls it; and so I rushed to my room to have a big cry; for, don't you see, my dear, that my glowing hopes were all dashed, that the sun of my morning had set in gloom?

From ma, I got all kinds of sympathy; and calling pa in, we held a "cabinet council," as the papers say. Ma was for having pa go and challenge Noall to fight, for she was sure he could whip the spruce Yankee; but pa says he didn't come here for any such purpose; and he knew that *that* man had too much *grit* in him to stir him up. He said the best way was to preserve a "dignified silence," becoming people of quality—that only the law would talk of revenge. His counsel prevailed; and we resolved to be proud and independent. After this, we found him promenading up and down the halls, his arms folded; and I *do* wish you could have seen him—he looked so much like the Old Duke. But he don't cease to swear awfully when he comes into our room, for his hopes of me are seriously injured, it is very apparent.

Do you ask about Mr. Noall? The wretch! He never sent one word of apology to me, and did not show himself, doubtless being afraid of meeting pa. After tea, I could not restrain my curiosity to learn what came of the adventure with Miss Stanley; and I was almost dying to know what his familiarity with that lady meant. I should surely think, if he kissed *my* lips, and put *my* hands in his bosom, that it meant *something;* and don't you think so too, dear? So I stole out into the parlor, looking out upon the piazza, where Miss Stanley usually sat; and there, sure enough, I saw her and Mr. Noall, sitting on a *tête-à-tête*, in a low conversation. I could not be mistaken; they were talking in confidence; and his excited manner, and her evident earnestness, told the whole truth and nothing but the truth. The true English blood flew through my veins furiously, or as pa would say, like hot tallow into the molds, and with true courage, I resolved to hear for myself. So I stole up to the window close by them, and, shrouded in the curtain, was perfectly safe from being seen. What did I not hear! Gracious me! Would that I could forget it! My ears tingle; my heart is like a boiling caldron, almost running over; and what I have told pa makes him so mad I really fear he will break down under it.

"Ah, but you were *very* harsh and cruel to me!" said Miss Stanley. "You not only got angry for nothing—for the young man who took me to the Chestnut street Theatre was Cousin George, from the West—but you went so far as to flirt with that poor English girl"—(*poor* English girl! Just think of that insult, my dear!)—"and made yourself rather notorious for the exclusiveness of your devotion to her. *This* I call trifling; and, if it was to punish me, it was done, not only to my unhappiness, but, I fear, to the unhappiness of another, whose simplicity" —(think of *that* insult, my dear!)—"Ought to have protected her from your advances." All this she said to him in a quiet manner; and I longed to reach out and pull her nasty hair for the epithets she bestowed upon your own Rosa Matilda.

But, if I was angry at *her* speech, what do you think I was at his? The brute! Just hear what *he* said: "I own that I was hasty; and I ask and pray for your forgiveness. I was told that the person at the theatre with you, and with whom you seemed so familiar, was a lieutenant in the army; and I was fired with jealousy that you should show *any* but me such civilities. It was *very* wrong, I knew. It was at that moment that I made the rash resolve to punish you by boldness and flirtation, and have therefore followed you the rounds, only studying means to drown my own chagrin; for, my dear Emma, I knew I was doing you injustice, and wanted to say so, but could not. It was that which made me seize upon that silly English girl"—(Heavens! My very teeth gritted like a crazy woman's at *that* speech. Silly! Just think of it!) —"and to flirt with her. She and her parents are such consummate snobs, and so ignorant of everything American, that I thought the lesson they might learn from an experience or two of the proper kind could do them no hurt. I never did the silly young woman any harm, I am sure. If I did, I can repair it by calling on them to-morrow with Lord Napier, who, you know, is to have rooms next to ours, to-night."

I waited to hear no more, and flew to tell pa all I had heard; and he has been furious ever since. Ma is completely stricken, and says we must leave, to-morrow, after breakfast, before Napier is out, else we shall be subjected to still greater mortification. So, while ma is packing, I write to you to tell you how *very* sick I am of this whole country and the people. Of one thing I am very certain—these people are just as sharp as we English; and, when we think we are great "lions," they are only making fun, and see through our pretensions as easily as any Englishman could. I do think Dickens was, as the Americans say, "greatly humbugged"—what a funny word!—and that they laughed in their glasses at his pretension as much as they laugh at pa's. Poor pa! He will not be called *Sir* Tudor any more.

I have learned a great deal by travelling; and I am sure none of us will put on airs any more. We shall travel hereafter in a respectable way, but give ourselves no trouble about trying to appear among the best. To-morrow morning, we leave for Boston, where pa will make a heavy purchase of tallow, for he says the market here, like us, is "down;" and he is going to invest. So we shall make more money than will cover our expenses.

We shall return by the 15th of August steamer. I don't like to go to New York again, but suppose I must, for it is there we take the steamer. When I get home, how much I shall have to talk about! For Heaven's sake, don't say anything about my love affair to pa's clerk! for *now* I am bound to have him; and I guess ma will not interfere any more. I always did like him; but you may keep it all to yourself. Prepare, my darling, to see your friend about the 28th. Until then, think over kindly the sorrows and joys of your ever dear

ROSA MATILDA TALLOW.

LUCY IN THE CITY.

LUCY IN THE CITY.

CHAPTER I.

THERE, now, mother, I am almost ready to sit down and tell you all about it. I had to run out and milk Sukey first. She was *so* glad to see me! and so were the chickens and old Brownie—but not more glad than I was to see them. Three weeks seem to me like an age. Let me put away those tea-things—oh, no, I'm not too tired!—and then we will sit down in the door; and you may knit, and I'll talk—and peel those apples too, for the pies to be made in the morning.

Well, you know father saw me safely in the cars after we got to Jacksonville, and put my ticket in my hand to give the conductor. After he had shaken hands and gone out, I felt almost like—crying at being left alone among so many people, and the bells ringing, and the locomotive screaming—such a horrible noise, mother! You never heard it, did you? But, after the cars were once in motion, I grew quite composed, for no one seemed to mind me; and I felt quite exhilarated by the rapidity with which we flew along.

I suppose you thought I looked very nicely when I set out—didn't you, mother?—with the black silk dress which we had made over, and my bonnet newly bleached and trimmed. I'll confess *I* thought I was rather smartly dressed; but, when I came to compare myself with the ladies whom I saw about me, I found that coat-sleeves, and bonnets large enough to shadow one's face, were out of date; and when I heard a handsome girl in the opposite seat whispering "Antediluvian," with a very amused and sarcastic face, I supposed she meant me, and blushed and fidgeted awhile, but finally concluded not to mind it.

Every little while the train would stop at stations; and people would get on, and others off the cars; so that I had enough to keep me interested. The women looked very queer, the most of them. I could not imagine what *was* the matter with them, and finally studied it out that they had on some kind of car life-preservers; so that, if there was a collision, they would be in less danger of being crushed. This made me uneasy, because I had none; yet they looked so ugly, that I was almost willing to run the risk of one ride without such a preserver. By and by, I began to grow uneasy about uncle's being at the cars to meet me. I did not know what to do in case he should be kept, for I had forgotten the number of his house, which he had been so particular to give me. So when the conductor came for my ticket, I asked him if he knew Ebenezer Wilmot, and, if he did, if he would please to tell me what the number of his residence was. He smiled, and said that he did not recollect him. I told him I thought he must know him, for he had lived in New York a great many years, and that his house was in Union Place; but I had forgotten the number. He replied that there were a great many persons in the city; and he was not personally acquainted with all of them. Again I saw the young lady opposite me smile, and look at me from head to foot. I am sure I thought it rather strange that he should never have heard of an old citizen so wealthy and respectable as Uncle Eben. So I asked him, then, if my uncle was not at the station waiting for me, if he would see my trunk safely out of the baggage-car, and put it with me into an omnibus, describing the trunk to him as well as I could; but he seemed in haste to get away, and told me to give my checks to an omnibus man; and he would attend to my baggage, and drive me where I wanted to go.

I was just as uneasy on the subject as ever, when the train stopped, and everybody jumped from their seats, and caught up their shawls, carpet-bags, bundles, babies, etc., and I with the rest—though, mercy, it didn't seem as if we could be half way to New York yet! Only four hours to come almost a hundred miles! Old Brownie wouldn't have carried us more than sixteen miles, and would have thought that he had done well, then.

I got all mixed up in the crowd, and had to go along, whether I wanted to or not, though I tried to stop, and look about for my uncle, and to go and see about my trunk. "Please don't push me so," I said to a large, fat woman, who was almost running over me. "I want to go back, and get my trunk."

"Run along, you little fool! You'll find your trunk on the ferry-boat," was her polite rejoinder. And I did as I was bid, because I could not do anything else. Sure enough, when I got on the boat that takes the passengers over into the city, I saw a monstrous wagon full of baggage; and, going up, I gave the man my check; and he set my trunk off; and I sat down on it to keep it safe. I was glad enough to see uncle's smiling face, the moment the boat touched the wharf; and it did not take him long, with his quick, keen eyes, to find me out. "Ah, ha, little daisy; here you are, fresh from the clover fields!" he cried, as he came up and kissed me right before everybody; but I was so glad to see him again, I'm sure I didn't care. "I meant tc have come down early enough to cross over, and meet you at the cars. You were not afraid, were you?"

"A little, Uncle Eben; but I got along very well."

"Well, you're all right now, my dear. Got your baggage? Ah! this is all, is it? Here, Washington, put this in the carriage."

A negro man, dressed a great deal nicer than father is on Sundays, stepped forward, and picked up my poor little hair-trunk with a look of curiosity and contempt, which I saw very plainly. "Better get a cartman tote dis trash," I heard him grumble under his breath. "Massa has no respeck for de position of his coachman."

Uncle helped me into his carriage; and we were driven along at a cautious rate through *such* a jam. Why, I expected we should be run into on every side! We went through Broadway, that you and I have read so much about. The noise, and crowd, and splendid buildings were more than I had expected; and, though we were more than an hour reaching the house, I was not a bit tired. I should not have known whether we had been on the way one hour or ten, I was so absorbed in *looking*, and in listening, too, for dear uncle talked all the way, and explained everything.

I was almost afraid to go up the fine marble steps, when we at last got out of the carriage. You've never been at Uncle Eben's, have you, mother, since he had his last house built? It seemed as if even my best morocco slippers were not nice enough to step upon the carpet in the parlors. I thought of the rag one which you and I made with so much labor, and were so pleased with when we got it down in the front room. Uncle rang a bell; and a mulatto girl came to the door.

"Show Miss Wilmot to her room; and help her to anything she wants," he said.

Miss Angeline looked at me from head to foot, and was about to giggle; but, catching her master's eye, she suddenly grew more polite. "Step dis way, if you please," she said. And, as I followed her, uncle told me that, by the time I had rested a few moments, and washed the dust from my face and hands, tea would be ready.

My chamber was almost as nice as the parlor—the most beautiful curtains, and carpet, and chairs, and a great mirror, and so many little things on the toilet table which I did not know the use of. The colored girl stood in the centre of the room, and watched me as I took off my bonnet and gloves, and then made a show of putting them away for me; but I could see very well that she thought me a great curiosity. I began to feel that I *was* a worse ignoramus than I had supposed; but I did not choose to be laughed at by a servant; so I sat down, and looked at her, a moment, quite steadily, and then told her she might leave; I did not need her services at present.

"Well, ring when you do, mum. I suppose you know dat by pulling dis here circumfluous knob, you cause de ringing to divert my attention from de regions I may be occupyin'."

And, with a superb courtesy, she backed out of the door, which she could not get through with one effort, she was so puffed and swelled out with that mysterious arrangement which had attracted my attention in the cars, and which I now saw could not be a life-preserver.

I brushed the dust off me, and bathed my face and hands, and smoothed my curls, taking pains to have them very nice, because I knew uncle liked them. I could see my whole figure in the mirror; and I must confess I was not quite so contented with my old black silk as I was when I left home. The girl had on a better one, and a dozen little fixings besides, that *I* should have thought good enough for a party. However, there was no help for it; and I was glad that Uncle Eben was an old bachelor, and had no finnified wife and daughters to be mortified at their country cousin. "I will stay altogether in the house," I thought, "and not put him to the blush by my ignorance of city fashions. *He* will like me just as I am." Comforted by this conclusion, I went down into the parlors, and found him awaiting me, sitting in a great velvet-cushioned chair. He pulled me into his lap, just as if I was still a little girl. "Little

Daisy's curls are as bright as ever, and her eyes and her cheeks," he said, pinching my face until I am sure it must have been rosy enough. "That comes of milking the cows, and running in the meadows, and living on peaches and cream, I suppose; hey, little girl?"

"I suppose it does, uncle. Just look at my hands, how brown they are! But why do you call me little? I am seventeen, now."

You ought to have heard him laugh! I grew quite confused, and was afraid he would think me foolish.

"You are, are you? And I'm not to call you my little puss, or my little daisy, or my little Lucy any more? You *have* grown tall since I saw you. But you are not so very large yet. Bless you, you are not a young lady, I hope! I hate young ladies. If you had a hoop on, now, I could not have you in my lap, nor get near enough to you to kiss you."

"What is a hoop, uncle?"

"Bless my soul! A hoop? Why, it's a prodigious circle, an immense balloon—bones—crinoline—a skeleton—a what-not—a—in short, a petticoat of a new fashion. Don't you take the magazines? I'll show you what it is to-morrow, when we go out to walk. I'll show you crinoline in perfection."

"Was that a hoop that made your servant look so like a big yellow pumpkin with a little black stem, uncle?"

"Yes, my dear. The encroachments of the other sex upon our rights are getting to be intolerable. Yesterday, I happened to get squeezed in between two ladies in an omnibus; and only a small part of my nose was visible. I was afraid I would never come to light again; but one of the fair ones departed; and I emerged to view much to the surprise of an old lady who was sitting opposite. 'Sakes alive!' she exclaimed; 'was you in there?' And then the men laughed; but the women did not blush. They do not know how, now-a-days."

I laughed, too, at Uncle Eben's story, and at his railing at the women; and then we went into his library, where he had ordered the tea to be served; and we had a cozy supper all to ourselves, with only one waiter, who did not embarrass me much. I believe my dear mother has taught me the *principles* upon which politeness is founded; and, for the rest, I used my wits and my eyes, when there was anything new.

I had a delightful evening. Uncle offered to take me to the opera, or to see the Ravels; but I was too tired to care to go out the first night; so he showed me over his house, and played the piano for me, told me the names and subjects of the beautiful pictures on the walls, and did all he could to amuse me. I do think he is the best old bachelor uncle in the world, mother; don't you?

Before I left him for my room, he told me that he had invitations out for a party, to come off the very next evening. He said he had asked me to come at this time on purpose to have me present; and he had made it a fancy dress party in order to have me play the character which he had chosen for me. It was the first party since his acquaintances had come back from the watering-places; and he meant to have it very fine.

"Oh, uncle!" I cried, in dismay, "I shall never be able to meet so many people! And I have no dress that is fit. Indeed—indeed, I must keep hidden in my room!"

"You must do nothing of the kind. Your name is on the cards of invitation. I made the ball on purpose for you. Have you no festival dress at all in that little hair-trunk you brought?"

"Nothing but a white mull that has been done up a dozen times. It is tucked; and I thought it very pretty before I came here. Mother ironed it nicely for me; but I am sure now, uncle, that you would not let me wear it."

"Yes, I will, and shall insist upon it. It is just what I expected you would have; and I should have been disappointed if you had fixed up anything more splendid. There, puss, you begin to look tired and a little sleepy. Go to bed, and dream that you will be the prettiest girl at the ball to-morrow."

I should have thought he was quizzing me if I had not known that he really loved me, and would not hurt my feelings for the world. So I kissed him good-night, and went to bed, but not to sleep for some time. I was excited by my journey, what I had seen, and what I had got to see. However, I was awake in the morning, and up and dressed two hours before I heard any stir in the house; and I had grown actually hungry before breakfast was served.

After breakfast, I saw some preparation, but not half so much stir as we should have made for a common tea party. The waiter was busy with the silver and glass in the dining-room;

and the parlors were being dusted, and some fancy lights arranged; and I suppose there was an extra servant or two in the kitchen.

About eleven o'clock, uncle asked me if I did not want to go down town, and do a little shopping, saying he would like to show me the fashionable stores; and we might stop at the Dusseldorf Gallery on our way back. I told him that you had given me ten dollars for spending-money; but I had not decided what I should get with it yet. I had just had my bonnet bleached and trimmed, and was not really in need of anything.

"Not in need of anything!" he exclaimed. "I wonder if there is another woman in the city so well off as that! You'll make a good wife for some man, my dear. But run, and put on that aforesaid bonnet which has been 'bleached and trimmed'—how many times, Daisy?"

"Three, Uncle Eben. But I do not like to go out with you. You have so many fine acquaintances; and you will be so ashamed when you meet them, with such a queer, old-fashioned little girl by your side!"

"Who told you you were queer and old-fashioned? Have you found that out already?

Well, your waiting-maid, Angelina, is a very good imitation of my *bon ton* lady friends, in the way of dress, and manners, too, perhaps. Do you already aspire to be like her? When I am ashamed of my rustic blossom, she shall first have given me some real cause."

I thought if uncle, who knew so well, didn't care, that I needn't; and so I tied on my bonnet quite gaily; and we started out.

I wonder if all old bachelors are like uncle, mother?—he has such strange ways of saying things, and is so sarcastic, sometimes, in spite of his good nature and his real kindness. I hardly knew what to make of his talk, at first, as we went along, I stumbling over people, almost, in my eagerness to use my eyes; but at last I entered into the spirit of it, I guess.

"So we are going a shopping, are we?" he begun. "I've a little silly female friend, a married lady, who informs me that shopping is quite an art, much cultivated and prized by her associates; and, from what I have observed, I should think it must be so. In fact, I should think it might almost be called one of the fine-arts. As our fair ladies are not altogether destitute of talent, and have no other means of exhibiting it, it is natural that they should seek the only avenue open for a useful and agreeable employment of the faculties which their Creator has bestowed. Upon every fine day, you will see the most fashionable thoroughfares of the city brilliant with the gay creatures, fluttering about, happy in their favorite pursuit. They purchase, and purchase, and purchase everything recommended by the ineffable young men making their *ko-tows* (that's Chinese for grand salaams, my dear) behind the counter, until their purses are emptied, and the patience of their husbands exhausted; but this does not dampen their ardor in the least. Yesterday, I overheard two elegant creatures conversing something in this wise:

"'What do you propose buying to-day, my dear?'"

"'Oh, I do not know, my sweetest! I spent all my allowance yesterday. But we can *look* at the lovely things, you know. And, if the merchants get out of patience, we can purchase a skein of silk or a spool of floss.'

"'But you know they never get out of patience. I spent four hours, the other day, looking at the dear, delicious laces and shawls at

Alltherage's, after I had mine for the season; and I took nothing; yet that elegant Slimwaist, who shows them, smiled as graciously when he bowed me out as when I came in. What white teeth he has! hasn't he? Let's go in there now. I heard, last evening, that some charming tissues had arrived. By the way, love, I have been told something so curious!—that the spines of shopkeepers were made of caoutchouc, and their tempers of the same.'

"'Ah, how queer! I've got some tissue paper stuffed in my purse, and some gilt buttons.'

"'Oh, it's so agreeable to shop! I wish there was nothing else in the world to do. But I must be home in three hours. My husband is going to Europe; and he asked me to be at home to dinner, to bid him good bye. It's such a bore to bid your friends farewell!'

"'Husbands are getting to be so exacting!'

"I tried to lag, so as not to be compelled to play listener; but, as they warmed with their subject, their own steps lessened; and I do not know how much I might have gathered, if I had not turned aside in desperation, and darted into a bazaar, where I stumbled among a whole crowd of butterflies fluttering about a garden of gay tissues, and Slimwaist himself, thrown into an admiring attitude, gazing ecstatically upon a strip of faded leaf-colored *something*, which he had gathered into airy folds, and was gently waving to display its beauties. I felt almost tempted to advise him to don the airy vesture he so elegantly recommended, and so fully appreciated; but, upon glancing at the slight moustache, whose glossy curves it would have been a pity to sacrifice, I refrained, and made my exit, encountering at the door the lovely feminines to whose soft conversation I had unwillingly been a confidant. I do not know if these beautiful creatures have ever heard that 'time is money.' If so, they must pay a double price for what is already dear enough. My friend, Bulbul I call her, describes the fascinations of shopping as irresistible—quite equal to the catching of husbands—and a good substitute for every sensible employment; and I take the sweet lady's word for it, and tell you as 'twas told to me, my artless Daisy."

We had now got down into a more crowded part of the city; and he was obliged to cease preaching; but his air was so funny, when he imitated the ladies, that I could not help laughing. "There, uncle! I suppose these are some of your patrons of shopkeepers," I said, as a couple of women fluttered past us, with their purses hanging from their fingers, and little bouquets on the back of their heads for bonnets, and flounces that spread out like a wide-open fan. You ought to have seen them, mother. Uncle told me they had a thousand dollars' worth of finery apiece upon them, just for a morning promenade. "They bowed to you, didn't they?"

"Yes, Lucy; I expect to meet half my lady friends out, this morning, making some last purchases for my ball to-night. The cards have been out ten days; and they regard it as a great affair. But don't be afraid of their knowing you. They think Miss Lucy Wilmot is a very different person; and, besides, they cannot see your face in that bonnet."

"Oh, uncle!" But he did not heed my tone of reproach.

"Here, puss, here we are at Stewart's. We'll go in, and look at the things. They will be very polite to me, and not expect you to buy. I don't suppose you would find it possible to expend all your money in so small an establishment, if you felt disposed."

It was so much like a fairy palace, that I forgot to be embarrassed by the splendid things or the splendid persons about me, any more than as if they had been enchanted people that I was seeing by the light of Aladdin's lamp. I followed Uncle Eben from department to department, and examined things it took my breath away to hear the price of. When we were looking at the silks, I saw one piece of small blue and white plaid that was *so* pretty. I almost sighed for the power to purchase it. It looked almost modest enough for my small means. I just said to uncle that I thought it sweet. "That would certainly be becoming to my little girl," said he, and ordered the salesman to cut off a dress pattern; and, while I was wondering what it meant, he took out his purse, and paid for it. I expect I looked delightful, for he laughed, and called me a true child of Mother Eve. Oh, dear, but didn't I want to ask him if it could not possibly be made up by evening! But I did not dare to. "What makes so many ladies look at me?" I asked, when at last I came to my senses enough to feel self-conscious.

"I suppose it's because your dress is small, and your bonnet large, and your sleeves tight, Daisy."

"But why do you want me to wear such a dress to-night, uncle?"

"Oh, it's just a whim of mine! Nobody will find fault with it, be sure. My distinguished niece, Miss Lucy Wilmot, is going to act in the character of the 'Country Girl,' you know."

I wanted to visit the Gallery; but, as we were rather later than we expected, and uncle had to go somewhere to see about his bouquets for the vases and tables, we were obliged to defer it. You're a little sleepy, aren't you, mother? and I am, too; so I'll tell you about the party in the morning.

CHAPTER II.

WHEN we got back to the house, I asked Uncle Eben if he did not wish me to do something to be useful. I told him I was a first-rate cake-baker, and would make some for him, if he desired. He said he had ordered everything from his confectioner's; I might tell him where the flowers would look best when they should come; but he could not think of anything else I could do.

Toward night, there were half-a-dozen elegantly dressed gentlemen made their appearance in the hall; and I thought, at first, that it was some of the party folks come unexpectedly early; but they turned out to be waiters supplied by the confectioner. About an hour afterward, uncle called me to look at the table which had been set in the dinning-room by these assistants. I wish you could have seen it, mother! It would have made our pumpkin-pies blush, and put our best frosted seed-cake out of countenance. Our roast turkeys might have held their own, though, I guess. There were plenty of delicate dishes of which I did not know the name, and beautiful ornamental devices. The table glittered with silver, and crystal, and china; and there were beautiful flowers which came from the hot-house, and cost more than I dare tell you. The gas was lighted in all the burners, to try the effect upon the table; and the genteel serving-men were standing in critical attitudes surveying it.

"Oh, how beautiful!" I exclaimed. "But, uncle, it is really getting dark out of doors; and I have not begun to dress yet."

"It's just six o'clock," said he, looking at his watch. "We've had nothing but a lunch since breakfast. There's a cup of coffee and a quiet little dinner waiting for us in the basement dining-room. Let's go down and refresh ourselves. You can eat in peace, little one, and take a siesta afterward. Not a guest will we see until ten o'clock."

"Why, uncle," said I, laughing, "I shall be ready for bed by that time! Why don't you have your party the next day after the one set?"

"There's only one sin more deadly than being out of fashion, and that's to be poor, my dear. It's the fashion to try and be the last at an assembly. I'm the only one in my circle that dares to do as he pleases. They call me vulgar, strange, an old fogy, absurd, ridiculous, etc.; but I am very rich, little one; and so they smile upon my 'bachelor's whims,' and pat my rough coat as if it were the sleekest silk that any lady's lap-dog ever wore. The belles are teasing me, now, to move further up town, perhaps with the hope that some one of them may be invited to become the mistress of the new establishment. *Then* wouldn't they put poor Uncle Eben under their dainty thumb, and make him keep his place?"

"I shouldn't like to live in the city, I believe," I said.

"And I wouldn't like to have you, my little Daisy. Now, if you have finished your dinner, you may go to your room, and sleep an hour, for you must be tired with the excitements of the day; and I do not want you to look sleepy by and by. I will have Angelica call you at eight o'clock; and you can be down before nine; for I know it doesn't take *you* half a night to make your toilet. There is neither arsenic, nor rouge, nor lily-white, padding, India-ink, or belladonna upon *your* toilet-table. You don't require much making up. Only be sure and get down where I can criticise your appearance before the guests begin to arrive."

I kissed him, and went up-stairs. I guess Uncle Eben does not know as much about the feminine heart as he thinks he does, if he expected me to sleep on the eve of such a grand affair, and my first appearance in city society. I was so excited that I could not close my eyes; and, as soon as Angelica went out of the room, I sprang off the bed, and, going to the wardrobe, took out my dress, and spread it on the bed, with all the articles I expected to wear. I could not help thinking they looked very pretty. I had bought a new blue waist-ribbon, and one for my hair.

After awhile, I took my hair down, and stood brushing it out a long time; then I curled it into long curls, two rows, all around my head, the way you like it best, mother; then I put on my checked stockings, and kid slippers, my ruffled dimity petticoat, and, lastly, my mull dress, that my kind mother had ironed so nicely that it looked as fresh as new. I fastened my sash with that little pearl buckle you gave me on my last birthday, twisted the ribbon through my curls, and, by the time Angelica came to call me, I was ready to go down.

I found Uncle Eben lounging on a sofa, sound asleep. So I stole around, and looked at the beautiful rooms all brilliantly lighted up, and then came back, and pinched him awake. "Will I do?" I asked, as he arose and rubbed his eyes.

"Fair as a snowdrop! You will do, exactly. I will tell you, now, how to behave. Just stay by my side until the company are pretty well gathered in, and act your own modest little self; that's all. Everybody else here, to-night, will assume a character. You have only to retain your own. Now, sit down here, and tell me how you have passed the time since I paid you that flying visit, last year. I see, by your flushed cheeks, that you are a little flustered. Take time, now, and keep steady."

I was just in the midst of our winter's singing-school, when the bell rang, and we heard people fluttering softly up and down the stairs. Pretty soon, they began to be announced. Oh, dear, there's no use trying! I cannot tell you half the people who were introduced to me in the next two hours—about all the characters we have ever read of—kings, queens, shepherdesses, Paul Prys,

gipsies, Nights, Mornings, Joan of Arcs, fairies, crusaders, belles of every century, Oberons, Titanias, and Billy Bottoms. Dresses more magnificent and persons more beautiful than I ever dreamed of, were there. Everybody smiled upon me, and said something pleasant to me; and, by and by, I forgot all about my own dress and appearance, and just abandoned myself to enjoyment. The sweetest music began to play; and a young gentleman, dressed as a Scottish chieftain, came and asked me to dance. I smiled, and asked him if it was the Highland Fling, and then told him I must refuse him, because I could dance nothing but country dances.

"But will you not lay aside your rustic ignorance for a little while, and dance one polka with me, Miss Wilmot?" he asked.

"I assure you I never danced a polka in my life," I answered, gravely.

"Well, I cannot say I am sorry to hear it, for I never admired the French thing," he answered. "But I should really like to dance with you, and wish you would engage yourself to me for the first old-fashioned dance of shepherds and milkmaids that is played."

I thought him a little bold, to say the least, in talking about my rustic ignorance; but he seemed so unconscious of saying anything improper, that I forgave him. He looked a real chieftain, tall and athletic, honest and handsome, too. I promised him my hand for the first set of cotillions that was made up.

"I'm glad you are getting acquainted with that Scotchman. You and he will like each other," said uncle to me, a little while afterward.

"Is he really a native of Scotland?" I asked.

"Not quite so much as you are of the rural districts, Daisy. He is a young lawyer here, a sensible fellow, the only young man in town that I care much about. He detests the women almost as heartily as I do."

"That *is* a recommendation in my eyes," I laughed.

"Do you see," continued uncle, in a low tone of voice, "that couple playing Beauty and the Beast? They were married last week. Don't you think the bride looks happy?"

"For my part," I said, "I not see any emotion—not a blush, nor a smile."

"Ah, you little rustic! don't you know that blushes and tears are out of fashion among people of the world? An emotion would ruin a woman's position. She looks rather self-satisfied, however, and has reason to. Almost any of these beautiful creatures that you see about you would have been glad to secure the Beast for a husband. She knows they are dying of envy."

"But why do the young ladies admire him?" I asked. "To me, begging your pardon, he looks rather old and very ugly."

"To tell you the truth, he *is* a little old, and has false eyebrows, and dyes his whiskers and hair, and was quite wild until he grew tired of it, and is now inclined to be an invalid the most of the time. But his family is an old family among us—has the butterfly spots upon its wings. Yea; and so has the Beast gold in his purse."

"What a pity!" I whispered, looking at the handsome young wife.

"Pity! I hope you do not suppose she needs pity? She will have what she loves. Her affections are not wasted. She loves diamonds better than kisses, and to be envied better than a young husband. She will have peacocks made of jewels upon the terraces of her country-house on the banks of the Hudson."

Here a young man attired as Beau Brummell sauntered up to us. "What a consummate actress you are, Miss Wilmot!" he drawled, with a smile which he intended to be very flattering. "Permit me to say that I have not seen a character performed so enchantingly to-night. I could almost fancy that you were the blooming country lassie which you personate."

"Indeed, I am nothing else, sir!" I answered, looking to uncle for relief; but he had turned away, purposely, I believe.

"He! he! he!" he tittered, as if I had said something very witty; "pre-cise-ly! What delicious music that is! Fair milkmaid, will you polk?"

"Will I *what?* Excuse me; I do not understand you."

"He! he! he! excellent! I forgot that it was not to be expected of you, this evening. Never mind. I hope to have the exceeding pleasure some time—aw!"

He made me so low a bow that I felt constrained to drop him a courtesy. So everybody had something to say to me, and everybody smiled at everything I said, no matter how seriously I spoke it.

After a while, I danced the cotillion with the Scottish chief. When it was finished we went and sat down in an alcove. "You look *really* amused and pleased," he said, looking at me with curiosity. "And—do you know?—I could wish that you *really* were what you seem to be to-night. *Then* you might not have lost the capacity of being made happy by simple things—much simpler things than this costly ball. If we could preserve the exquisite sensibility of our childhood along with our grown estate, how unnecessary it would be to pamper our palled appetite upon such epicurianism! A midnight banquet, where purple wines bubble up in glittering goblets, and a rich feast is on the board, where women stake the brightness of their eyes against the brightness of their jewels, and where chandeliers shed down a mockery of the day, cannot bestow a delight so deep and perfect as a walk in early spring-time in search of daisies and anemones, where the goblet from which you drink is the brook that sings, even while you quaff its cup of cold water:

" 'I steal by lawns and grassy plots;
I slide by hazel covers;
I wave the sweet forget-me-nots
Which grow for happy lovers.

" 'I slip, I slide, I gloom, I glance
Among my skimming swallows;
I make the nettled sunbeam glance
Against my sandy shallows.'

But daisies are old-fashioned. So are walks by the brookside. Some country damsels and their swains may not have entirely deserted the bespangled meadow and the bubbling waters; but they have gone from the hearts of the world's people. Rusticity rests upon blue violets and brooks. The ocean is still in favor; for the ocean is grand, majestic, overwhelming, an old aristocrat; and those who go to enjoy his society can be lodged in palatial hotels, and are not called upon to resign in his favor their waltzes, their flirtations, their gauze dresses, their fine horses, or their good dinners. All these necessary things are closely associated with their love of his grandeur, their appreciation of his sublimity. All the enthusiasm permitted to a refined nature may be expressed in his behalf without exciting a pitying smile. One of 'our own' poets, whose lyre was modulated precisely to accord with the souls of those he has so long played for, says, only too truly—

" 'You lie down to your shady slumber,
And awake with a bug in your ear;
And your milkmaid who walks in the morning
Is shod like a mountaineer'—

impressing very clearly the dangers of rustic sentimentality. To these fastidious and ethereal beings,

> "'A sly flirtation,
> By the light of a chandelier,'

is the highest heaven to which they aspire. But I beg your pardon, Miss Wilmot; I am actually preaching at a fancy ball. I have made myself very stupid, no doubt, and will try and make some amends by attending you to the supper-room, with your permission. Now, if all nations could be as easily moved in one direction as their motley representatives now are toward the eating department!"

We joined the crowd which were pressing into the dining-room. It looked so queer to me to see such brilliant personages, courtly dames, princes, nymphs, pages, Pagans, and Christians, all engaged in eating, as if there was no other occupation in the world, that I had rather look and laugh than taste any of the dainties which my chieftain brought me. There was a fairy, a beautiful Titania, in an exquisite lace dress, that looked as if about to melt into mist, and with little silvery wings folded on her shoulders, eating salad, instead of sipping flower-dew. I saw a queen, glittering with diamonds, sitting down in a chance corner, with a great plate full of knick-knacks ; a sentimental cavalier was stuffing himself with cold turkey ; Othello was washing down his grief with champagne.

I must say, mother, I have seen more real good manners at one of our paring-bees than I saw there. You see, there was a great crowd; and some people were so afraid that they would get nothing, that there was actually a little of what I should call scrambling, going on. The ladies' appetites were not quite so dainty as their dresses; and—if I must own it—I was certain that more than one of the gentlemen took more wine than was good for them.

"A supper table is what I call your true leveller, a real republican institution," said my Scotchman. "There's Queen Elizabeth hobnobbing over a plate of comfits with Davy Crockett; and there's Ophelia consoling herself with an ice. Isn't this a pleasant and instructive scene, Miss Wilmot?"

I thought I detected a little sarcasm in his voice; but I answered him that I was very much entertained indeed, as it was all so new to me.

But he was not my only attendant. Everybody was very civil to me. "Was I enjoying myself? How pleased my uncle must be to have me in his house! he must be so lonely! Why could I not spent the winter with him? They hoped to have the pleasure of making my better acquaintance very soon. What a pretty character I had chosen! how becoming it was to me!" etc. etc.

Once and a while, Uncle Eben would contrive to get by my side; and then he would tap my cheek, and there would be such a quizzical twinkle in his eyes that I could see he was very much pleased about something. "Just as I expected," he said, once. "I see my little Daisy is in full bloom, to-night. Enjoying yourself, are you?"

When he had opportunity, he would point out and explain some of the dresses and characters to me. "Do you see that Sister of Charity?" he whispered, toward the close of the ball. "That is Mrs. ——, the lady patroness of all the charitable societies, benevolent institutions, etc., in the city. She spends her whole time doing good. Those who do know say that she fastens her sewing-girl down to the lowest price, and pays her washerwoman in cold victuals and old clothes. But it would be heresy to doubt her self-sacrificing virtue. Why, only lately she has organized a society among the ladies of her circle, called the 'Greenland Fan Society.' Through their exertions, a ship has been chartered, and a whole cargo of fans, dilapidated and otherwise, collected from their fair owners, and dispatched to Greenland, to relieve the poor sufferers there from the heat; and it is expected that fans will be found to be exceedingly useful in promoting comfort, civilization, and Christianity. Last winter, she distinguished herself, by her indefatigable industry, in procuring subscriptions to purchase flannel petticoats for the children of the South-Sea Islanders. But I cannot enumerate half her good works. She will do that for herself, if you are so fortunate as to make her acquaintance. There!" he whispered again, "do you see that person in the garb of a Persian poet, with a rose in his silken girdle, and a lute in his hand. That is one of our authors. He is coming this way, and will probably address you a complimentary ditty."

As he came up to us, he said: "Water is bright in the two wells that lie among the roses, when the stars are in the sky above them; and so are thine eyes, O maiden!"

"Honey is sweet," I replied, "and so is the breath of flattery; but it does not agree with all tastes."

"I will not offer it to thy innocent lips, sweet rustic," he replied; and, after a moment's pause, he added: "Have you ever perused any of my couplets upon society? Here is one of them: To be simply ridiculous is absurd; but to be supremely, inimitably ridiculous is sublime. Look about you, and see if it is not thus."

I presume I looked as puzzled as I felt. Do you see any sense in it, mother?

"What pretty little woman was that with the basket of flowers?" I asked Uncle Eben, as I saw he had had a long chat with her.

"Oh, that's my married friend whom I call Bulbul! She lets me into a great many of the secrets of her acquaintance. For instance, she has just told me that that dashing-looking creature there has not exactly a heart, but a bosom of steel, and that she stains her eye-lashes, and eats cologne-water on sugar to make her eyes brighter. She'll be around here, to-morrow, and get very intimate with you, I've no doubt. Well, she's welcome to make use of all the 'arts and wiles' that she discovers in my little Lucy."

And so the night passed away; and one by one, and dozen by dozen the gorgeous guests departed; and I stole to my bed a little before the hour at which I usually rise, to dream confused dreams, in which knights, fairies, flower-girls, and lords whirled all together in a dizzy waltz to the sweetest music. Wasn't it nice, mother? Oh, I did so wish you were there, that it quite marred my enjoyment!

Breakfast was quite ready when I got up *that* morning, for it was as much as nine o'clock. I was really ashamed of myself for such indolence. Uncle Eben was waiting for me at the breakfast-table. "The drama being played," he remarked, "I suppose the entertainment will conclude with a farce. Do you know what you've got to do to-day, little one? As soon as breakfast is over, you must go and have that blue silk fitted; then you must return and dress for calls. You will have a few hundred to-day."

"What shall I wear, uncle?"

"Oh, anything! The best dress you have. By the way, I have bought you a corded skirt, a kind of compromise between your present slimness and crinoline—just enough to keep you from total disgrace."

Uncle went with me to the mantuamaker's. "Don't you make that dress too low in the neck; if you do, I'll denounce you," he said to Madame ——, as we were going into a back room to take my measure.

She laughed and promised. Everybody seems to like uncle, he is so good-natured, even when he scolds.

When we came back, I went up-stairs to put away my bonnet; and, when I came down, I found uncle lying back in his chair, and laughing in a little low way. "Here's the morning paper," said he. "Read the following report of the 'Fancy Dress Ball at the house of our esteemed fellow-citizen, E—— W——, Esq.'—this paragraph in especial."

I cut it from the paper, mother, and preserved it to read to you:

"But the belle, *par excellence*, after all, was the accomplished and beautiful niece of the host, the fair Miss L—— W——, a stranger in our city, and now visiting at the house of her bachelor uncle. Her dress was simplicity itself, perfectly appropriate to the character she personated, that of a country maiden; and never were the words of the poet more enchantingly realized, that 'loveliness needs not the foreign aid of ornament.' No splendor of the toilet could have enhanced the brilliancy of that fresh complexion, or the brightness of those dark blue eyes. Her beauty is as piquant as it is fresh. She acted her part with a charming *naïveté*, never forgetting what was due to the rustic maiden; though the high-born grace of the lady still gleamed through the enchanting disguise."

But I have strung out my story until it is time to put the dinner up. This afternoon, I will finish it, dear mother.

CHAPTER III.

I FELT like crying when I had finished reading the paper; and I told Uncle Eben it was too bad to get a joke upon other people at my expense. He said "they had got it on themselves; and perhaps it would teach them a lesson; that I need not feel bad about it. I had been myself, and must continue to be so; and, if they did not like me as well when they found out that I was really a country girl, and not the accomplished heiress they had taken me to be, why, we could not help it. People need not jump at conclusions. Because he had said that a favorite niece was coming to see him, they must needs go to thinking that nothing but wealth and fashion could make her a favorite. The young men, doubtless, supposed I had made a will in your favor; and they would have said just as many fine things as they did, if you had been as homely as a mud fence. Never you mind, little one. The women may turn up their noses in secret at your dress and manners; but they will not dare to do it openly; and let me just hint to the marriageable young men that I think of adopting you, and my house will be besieged, and would be if you were cross-eyed and pug-nosed. I guess though there is one at least of the number, who can appreciate modesty, beauty, and true refinement, even where there is no 'foreign aid of ornament' to set it off."

Don't think me vain, mother, in repeating what he said. He just said it, I suppose, to cheer me up.

I concluded to make the best of it; so I put on the corded skirt, and my prettiest dress, next to the white; and made my hair look as well as possible, and reappered before my uncle to take my part with him in receiving visitors.

I was glad they came in crowds, for I did not have to say much; and it made it less embarrassing. But my eyes were opened now; and I could see the looks of surprise, disappointment, and mirth which were slily interchanged. My self-respect coming to the rescue, I was able to bear it very well. As for uncle, I could perceive that he was in the highest spirits; and I shouldn't wonder if some of the rest were sharp enough to see it, too.

Just at dark, my new dress came home. Uncle told me to go put it on, and he would take me to the opera. You've seen it, mother. How pretty it is made, with short sleeves and low in the neck! *I* thought it was too low; but uncle said "Pshaw! that was nothing!" I was going to don my leghorn bonnet: but he told me that we were to ride, and that I might just throw my veil over my head. "Here," he said; "first put these flowers in your hair."

I was dazzled, at first, by the lights and the display; but, after we had sat in our box a few moments, I began to take note of what was about me. The ladies and gentlemen were dressed as if for a party. I could not help blushing, mother, absolutely blushing, to see how some of the former were attired. I asked uncle if those were *respectable* women.

"The very condensed extract of respectability," was his reply. "Don't be alarmed, Lucy, at anything you may see. It takes so much to make the skirts of the dresses, now-a-days, that there is nothing left for the waist and sleeves."

"What are those queer little things they are all holding?"

"Telescopes, to discover the stars, my dear. I expect that you will be one of almost the first magnitude, to-night."

I felt very uncomfortable to see so many of the things pointed at me like so many pistols; and I wished uncle had taken seats in a less conspicuous place; but, when the overture, as they call it, began to play, I was so enchanted I forgot everything. It was the sweetest music I ever heard; and I almost imagined I was in heaven, I was so rapt in it. The glittering lights, the performers, the gay throng, all took on a magical effect, and seemed to be lifted up and floating away in an ethereal atmosphere. Then a woman, elegantly dressed, glided on the stage, and commenced a kind of half-speaking, half-singing, looking at us appealingly, as if she were in some trouble, and all of a sudden, as I was looking earnestly at her, her bosom began to heave; and she burst forth in a succession of trembling shrieks that made me jump to my feet in alarm. "Mercy! what is the matter with her?" I asked. But uncle pulled me down in my seat, and told me, a little sharply, not to make a goose of myself. I guess he was provoked at my stupidity, for he is very fond of the opera. I must say, mother, I had rather hear Jessie Clyde sing one of her ballads; but uncle tells me I will think differently one of these days, when my taste is more cultivated, and I learn to detect and feel all that the music expresses.

During recess, several people left their boxes, and came over to ours. Among them was Mr. Fitz Foom, the young gentleman who played Beau Brummell, at the party. He was excessively polite to me—didn't seem at all put out by the discovery that I was a country girl and didn't wear crinoline. I wish I could describe him to you, mother. He was small, and he was pale, and he was *nice*, oh, so nice! He had hands about the size of mine, covered with kid gloves, white as snow. He had a little bit of silky, light-colored moustache, pale blue eyes, and a face as expressive as a piece of paper with nothing on it. He looked as if he had just been taken out of a French bandbox, and smelt like a dying musk-rose. If you had seen him, so *dreadfully* dainty, holding his opera-glass—that's the telescope, as uncle calls it—and perfumed handkerchief, as if he was afraid to touch even them, you'd have felt like taking him across your lap, and spanking him, mother. He was such a contrast to Mr. Hamilton—he's the one who was my Highland chief—that he appeared more insignificant still. Mr. Hamilton was tall, and plainly dressed, and had no gewgaws about him. There was something deep and manly in his tone that made Mr. Fitz Foom's lisping little voice sound rather ridiculous.

"Wasn't you quite overcome by Mr. Fitz Foom's attractions?" asked uncle, as we rode home. "I assure you, they conferred a great deal of honor upon you."

"To tell the truth, dear uncle, I was thinking, the most of the time, what a splendid figure he would cut riding round the yard upon Sukey's horns. Oh, dear! wouldn't I like to invite him out in the country, and frighten him out of his five exquisite senses with a few little harmless tricks!"

"Good!" he laughed. "Perhaps we can bring it about, for—let me tell you a secret—the young gentleman is in love with you."

"With me! What do you mean?"

"Oh, I've not had my eyes in use for forty

years for nothing! He's in love—not with your eyes, or hair, or fresh young face, or modest, affectionate heart—but with your prospects; for I have slily insinuated to him that your father is worth fifty thousand, and that you were, of all my nieces, my favorite. You must forgive me, Daisy; but I wanted to see the result."

"Well, uncle, I must say you take great liberties with my good nature."

"It's nothing serious, my dear, just to be bothered with his attentions a week. It won't hurt you nor him."

I thought uncle was mistaken in his surmises; but the very next morning there came a beautiful bouquet, with the compliments of Mr. Fitz Foom.

"Poor Fitz Foom! I wonder if he got trusted for it?" remarked Uncle Eben. "I expect he needs a wife very much to pay his tailor's and perfumer's bills for him. The price of kid gloves is rising, too; and that's more fatal to his interests than a rise in the sugar market."

We had a great many calls that day, also. I got heartily tired of them. I wanted to sit in the library, and read some of the many attractive books I found there. If I did not love you, and father, and my old home so much, I should like to be Uncle Eben's housekeeper. That library is such a pleasant place! We breakfast in it; and then there are the morning papers and all the new books; and it has such a snug, comfortable look. There are pictures, and a case of minerals, and shells, and fossils, and a bust of Shakspeare, and so many interesting things.

In the evening, we went to see the Ravels; and there I *was* amused! It is worth a trip to New York. You've read about them, mother? They don't speak a word. All their playing 's done in pantomime. You and father *must* take a trip down to the city, some time, and see Uncle Eben, and the town, and the Ravels. What? You guess you'll have to be making visits there before long, if you want to see your daughter? Pshaw, ma! you'd better wait until uncle *asks* me to live with him. You was't thinking of uncle's asking? Well, wait till you hear about Mr. Fitz Foom, then.

For the next few days, we kept pretty quiet, for I wanted all my mornings to pass in the library. We took some delightful walks in the afternoons. Uncle Eben would take so much pains to explain things to me! I couldn't help noticing the little girls and boys that we met—miniature men and women. Their faces were as pale as flowers grown in a cellar; and they had the composed stare and preternatural self-possession of their elders, as well as the fine and expensive dress. I declare it made my heart ache to see them; and I longed to ask some of the pretty little girls to go home with me, and learn to slide down the straw-stack, climb the chestnut-tree, feed the chickens, and ride the pony. I don't believe they ever saw a ten-acre lot in their lives, or plucked a violet out of the grass, or ate mush and milk with the cream stirred in. I'm *so* glad I was not born a city child, for then I should have no such delightful recollections of playing in the farm.

I spoke about the children to uncle.

"Children!" said he, contemptuously; "there are none now-a-days. I used to love little girls above all things—the artless, willful, romping, modest, rosy little girls, in pantalets and pinafores. I could have sacrificed anything to them—my afternoon nap, or my smoking-cap to make a doll-baby of. They might have pulled my whiskers out, and spilled my ink on the carpet, and I wouldn't have winced. But *now*—humph!

A few nights ago, I was at an assembly; and it was nearly midnight when I first observed what I took to be a cunning puppet in imitation of the lady of the house—a little doll-like thing, in a dress with five flounces, with a bouquet, fan and lace handkerchief, a miniature of every mature grace, and the centre of an admiring circle. But what I took to be a thing of art was really not a puppet, but the daughter of the lady of the house, six years of age. She was bandying compliments with the ease of a woman of the world. Her mother introduced me. With that want of tact which makes me so absurd, I addressed her as if she had been an ordinary little girl—'My dear, are you not sleepy? "Early to bed," you know, etc.' Ah, I had lost all chance of ever being friendly with her, kindly as my intentions were! Her cheek flushed with disdain. 'I remain until after supper,' she replied, in the freezing tone so well calculated to check any further advances upon my part."

I don't always quite understand Uncle Eben. Once, when we passed a pompous-looking man, who bowed to him, I asked who he was.

"Oh, that," said he, "is a fine, portly old gentleman whom everybody esteems! He was lately the president of a company for the manufacture of gold coins out of gas. The shares rose so high that speculators had to go up in balloons to take them; but, unfortunately, the gas proved explosive, burst, and ruined the company. The coins fell into the laps of the directors; and the rest got nothing but the gas. The president, overcome by his misfortunes, immediately retired into a brown stone mansion on Fifth Avenue, and has abstained from any but the most exclusive society ever since. He has been much commiserated by his friends; and I think it helped him to marry off his daughter, the young creature we saw playing Beauty to the Beast, the other night. We all sympathize with adversity, you know."

"You are trying to puzzle, aren't you?" I asked.

"Maybe. But don't bother your innocent brains about it. Come in here, and I will buy you some bonbons."

We went into an elegant saloon.

"I used to think dissipation confined to my own sex," he continued; "but, if you had frequented this establishment as long as I, you would become convinced that we are not guilty of all that may be classed under that head. When I have seen fashionable mothers here at midnight, lavishing their smiles upon gentlemen *not* their husbands, and sipping luxurious refreshments, and have thought of their poor infants at home—abandoned to the tender mercy of Bridgets, as fond of a little stealthy enjoyment as themselves in a less refined way, and giving the helpless little ones anodynes to secure themselves leisure for an hour in the basement dining-room —I have shuddered at the picture conjured up. Do you wonder I do not marry? But mercy! whom am I talking to? My little Lucy must forget what I have said. Let her always keep her own affectionate heart and unsullied conscience, and believe that every one else is as pure as herself."

We met Mr. Fitz Foom in the saloon; and he asked permission to call in the evening, if we were not engaged out. My uncle told him we were *not*, and should be happy to see him—very happy. He looked delighted. Still, I saw him enjoy, with an indescribable, despairing glance, my morocco shoes and pink silk gloves. "He feels like a lamb about to be butchered, and is endeavoring to prepare himself for the sacrifice," I thought. "He will tell me how to dress in better taste when he acquires the right to instruct."

Mr. Fitz Foom was faithful to his engagement, coming in all milk-and-water smiles, perfumes, and politeness. I was so provoked, I didn't know what to do, when uncle got up and begged to be excused for half an hour to write an important letter.

He had not been out of the room over five minutes when Mr. Fitz Foom was on one knee before me, asking me to marry him. How it came about, I cannot tell to this day. He took me all of a sudden, before I had time to put on any precautionary reserve. He did it very prettily, with two fingers of his snowy hand pressed against the padding on the left side of his vest.

I was dreadfully embarrassed at first, and could hardly summon self-possession enough to draw away the hand which he attempted to take. But, as I looked down at the dainty creature, thrown into a studied attitude, and not one shade of doubt upon his expectant face, a little feeling of anger drew away timidity. But he was too insignificant for anger; and, when he murmured, rhapsodically, "Miss Wilmot, the happiness of a virgin heart, that has never hitherto breathed its affections upon earthly shrine, is hanging upon your lips," a vision of his "virgin heart," stuffed full of unpaid bills, arose before me, and I laughed.

"If your happiness is hanging upon my lips, I am afraid it will get a fall," I said. "I do not think there is any congeniality between us. I could not think of marrying you, Mr. Fitz Foom."

"Oh, I'm sure there is, Miss Wilmot! I have thought of nothing else since the first moment I met you."

"But I am a plain country girl" (he raised his hands in deprecation); "and you are an elegant man of the world" (here he smiled, and tried to look modest), "a kind of butterfly, 'roving from flower to flower.' Your hands are very white and soft, much more so than mine; and, if you married me, you would soon grow tired of country life. Besides, your wrists are not strong enough for milking; and I am resolved that the man I marry must milk all the cows."

His eyes opened wider than they ever had done before.

"But why need we live in the country at all? Of course, I should be afraid of the cows. They are horrid creatures. It was not my intention that we should reside"——

"But you see we cannot do as we please. I understand that you do not possess much available property yourself; and my fortune depends at present upon the will of my father. He wishes me to marry some one to take the charge of the farm off his hands. He is getting a little infirm with years, and would welcome a smart, capable son-in-law, who could guide the plough, take care of the stock, haul the grain to market, and oversee things generally. If you will promise to do this, I don't know—though it's rather sudden—but—perhaps"——

"Oh, I cannot accept you upon such terms!" he exclaimed, with an expression of horror, as he arose from his knee, and retreated a step or two.

"You would have to eat pork and boiled victuals in the kitchen along with the men, or else they would say you felt above them, and would refuse to work for you. One thing, though, would be nice—coming to town to sell our butter and eggs, and dropping in to Uncle Eben's to dinner."

"I should perish—of—disgust!" he murmured, in despair. "That certainly wouldn't pay. I couldn't think of it. I must bid you a very good eve"——Here the thought of a dun which was dogging him came over him, perhaps, and urged him back to another trial. "Re-ally, now, Miss Wilmot, why wouldn't your uncle give us a home here, and be done with it? It would be so agreeable all round."

"Well, I don't know. Perhaps if you should ask him, he would suspect you of mercenary motives."

"He would do me the greatest injustice, then, my angelic Lucy. I swear to you"——

"But it's wicked to swear."

"That, for your dear sake, I would go through"——

"The barnyard to drive up the cows for me to milk?"

"That without you I shall be a broken"——

"Down adventurer."

"I believe you mean to insult me, Miss Wilmot," he said, at this, retreating toward the door, just as it was thrown open for Mr. Hamilton to enter. I blushed; and Mr. Fitz Foom made a hasty exit.

Mr. Hamilton was constrained in his manners; and I was very glad to see Uncle Eben coming to the rescue. "Ha, Puss! you were rather saucy," he cried, as he came in. "But served him right! served him right! Bless my soul! but didn't the picture you drew frighten him?"

"Why, uncle! have you been"——

"Listening? Yes, the whole time. Little Daisy, here, has been trying to strike up a bargain with Fitz Foom, to tend her dairy for her, Mr. Hamilton."

"Oh, uncle!" I cried. And then I ran out of the room, and left them to themselves.

You are getting tired; aren't you, mother? Well, would you believe that, two or three days before I came away, Mr. Fitz Foom came back again, and was so good-natured and so insensible that I had to forgive him? He is determined not to give up the ship. I expect he's in very straitened circumstances. I felt like offering him the loan of my purse, with all my ten dollars of spending money. But I recollected that you needed a merino dress for winter; and, as Uncle Eben was as good as to buy me everything I wanted, I bought the dress for you; and uncle added the muff and tippet. Aren't they nice? He's such a dear, queer man; isn't he? Uncle Eben, I mean. I am so glad he has invited me to visit him, for, despite of all my blunders, I enjoyed myself so much, and saw so many new things; and Mr. Fitz Foom told me he was coming out to visit us before long—and—and—what makes me so red in the face. Why, I don't know but I am—but—Uncle Eben is coming out, next month; and he's going to bring Mr. Hamilton with him. He wants you to make his acquaintance, he thinks so highly of him—and—dear me, how warm it is here? Don't you think so, mother?

MR. FITZ FOOM IN THE COUNTRY.

A SEQUEL TO LUCY IN THE CITY.

DEAR UNCLE EBEN:

IT'S well that you are a hundred miles away from your indignant niece, if you want to save your hair from a most unmerciful pulling! What, in the name of sense, possessed you to send Mr. Fitz Foom out here to visit *me?* Knowing everything as well as you do, I must say that the joke was extremely practical, at my expense as well as his. Poor fellow! he left, this morning, after a visit of three days, having come, I understood, with the intention of remaining as many weeks.

Last Tuesday forenoon, as I was busy in the kitchen, for it was baking day, and I had a great deal to do, there came a knock at the front door. Supposing it to be some of the neighbors, I just slipped off my apron, rolled down my sleeves, gave my hair a dash down with my hands, and hurried to open it. Judge of my surprise, when there stood Mr. Fitz Foom, a jaunty little cloak and cap on, a little cane twirled in his fingers, and a smile upon his pretty little face, as exquisite a specimen of a small man as could be imagined! I was so taken aback that I could hardly ask him in, and could not forbear a sly glance at a long streak of flour which ornamented the side breadth of my gingham dress, and which I had gained in passing the flour-barrel on my last errand to the pantry. I saw him looking in the same direction; but he smothered any horror which he may have inwardly felt at this betrayal of my morning occupations.

"I suppose you received the note which I sent you by post announcing my intended visit, Miss Wilmot?"

No; I had not received it. I mutely wished that I had, when I thought of how little we were prepared for *such* company.

"You must pardon the very great liberty I have taken in accepting your uncle's invitation, who insisted upon my coming to see you without further ceremony than the sending of a note. He thought the country air would do me good, as I was complaining of dyspepsia. That my own heart pleaded with me to yield to his kind persuasions, I will not say, for I am forced to silence. I have sworn that, whatever that beating heart may feel, its emotions shall be kept secret from their fair and agitating cause. Do not blush, sweet being; I have come only as a friend."

I suppose you will call me a silly little girl if I confess that my face was redder than a pulpit-cushion for a minute or two; but his manner was so very impressive and overpowering, and his appearance so unexpected, that I was discomposed. I gave him as cordial a welcome as I could counterfeit. A queer look came over his face when he entered the keeping-room. He seemed a little afraid of hurting his patent leathers by bringing them in contact with the home-made carpet; and I saw the critical glance which he gave at father's favorite picture, the portrait of Washington, which hangs, you remember, over the mantel, with the china dog under it.

It was a splendid Indian-summer day; and *I* thought the room was very pretty. The sunshine came in the two front windows; and I had looped the curtains back with sprays of scarlet bittersweet, and made everything as neat as a pink. I gave him a seat by the window, and excused myself for a few moments, to go out and give mother warning of the unexpected guest. She laughed heartily when I told her that Mr. Fitz Foom had arrived with his carpet-bag; which relieved me, for I expected she would be vexed to death.

"Well, well, Lucy! who'd have thought it? I guess I shall not let you go to the city again. Never mind about the dinner, child. I'll get it on the table without further help. Go and put on your merino dress, and do the best you can to be polite to him."

I had made a nice custard, and set it to cool; and there was a plump pair of chickens in the oven; so I gave myself no uneasiness about the table. Ten minutes sufficed me in which to don my dress, smooth my hair, and put on a linen collar. When I returned to the keeping-room, there sat the visitor looking disconsolately out of the window, a very visible shade of disappointment upon his face. "You've a very pretty place here, Miss Lucy, but not at all what I expected from the description of your uncle. He gave me to understand that the house was a

Grecian villa, standing in the midst of a noble forest of oaks, with a park stretching away upon one side, and with out-buildings and gateways of the most tasteful and appropriate character," he remarked. "I could hardly persuade myself that I had been directed aright—not that everything is not very nice, indeed, but so different, you know, from what I had been led to expect."

"Uncle Wilmot has a very vivid imagination, Mr. Fitz Foom; and you must make allowance for its exercise. It's only one of his standing jokes, calling this a *Grease*-ian villa, because father raises so much pork. The out-buildings *are* 'appropriate' to the business, as you would think, if you should see all the pig-pens. He calls the hen-house an aviary, and the Shanghais foreign birds. The meadow is the park. As for the old oak-trees, he could not praise them too much."

The very slightest tremble of disgust disturbed the moustache upon his patrician lip as I spoke of the Grecian villa. It was a pun too horrible for him to contemplate, and for which you, dear uncle, must be solely responsible. He looked about, as if mutely asking for his hat, but, after a moment of troubled silence, regained a forced composure.

"And is pork-raising a *profitable* business, Miss Wilmot?"

"I believe it is regarded as such; but I cannot positively say."

"How much do you think—that is, has your father laid up any particular sum of money out of it?"

"I do not know just how much, Mr. Fitz Foom. And you must not think that it is his especial calling. My father is a farmer, who raises wheat and corn. But out of the refuge of his fields, he has enough to fatten a few droves. I suppose you know but little of the country, Mr. Fitz Foom?"

"Very little, indeed. I've been in it occasionally, for a day or two, with a party of friends, rusticating on the estate of some wealthy gentleman. I don't think I should like *the* country. It's very nice to talk about, but very vulgar close at hand. I don't see how so ethereal a being as yourself, Miss Lucy, could have survived so long in it. I trust that soon the persuasions of friends, of your uncle, and—and your humble servant, will induce you to forsake it?"

"My heart is wedded to it; it is my home; and I love it, sir."

"If we could wed that virgin heart to something better! he! he! he! But I will not again call up those divine blushes."

"The day is lovely; would you like to walk over the farm a little, before dinner, Mr. Fitz Foom?" I asked, anxious to escape from an eloquence so overwhelming.

I swung my straw hat on my arm; and we sallied forth. I noticed that he shivered a little in the cool, bright air, which only invigorated me, and made me feel mischievous, too, in my overflow of animal spirits. As we sauntered under the oaks, I gathered the most brilliant of the dropping leaves, and wove them in a wreath, with which I offered to crown his "Beebe's best;" but he was afraid of disturbing its gloss; and so I donned the garland myself, and laughed, without any more blushes, at his profuse compliments. Poor fellow! I suppose it's up-hill business to him, getting trusted for his new clothes; and I felt for him in the pains he took with his hat; and, when he split the knee of his pantaloons getting over the fence into the meadow, my condolences were sincere.

"It's the only pair I have with me," he said, with a rueful smile.

"Never mind! Mother will mend them for you, after you go to bed to-night, if you will put them out in the hall."

"But I never wore anything patched in my life."

"That will not need patching, only darning, which is not so bad; and everybody wears patched clothes in the country. Isn't it pretty from here—this meadow sloping away, and girdled about with that silver stream?"

"Charming! ah! very! good farm land, eh?"

"Very good for grazing and hay, sir."

"How many acres are there in your father's farm?"

"Three hundred. One hundred is grain land, one hundred pasturage, and one hundred timber. The pigs fatten themselves upon the acorns in the woods. The wheat is near to a good market; and the dairy is very profitable indeed. Do you see that cow down by the creek? She is mine, and my especial pet. She is worth five hundred dollars; and I'd rather have her than a set of pearls. Then I have all the money I can make from selling her butter, for pocket-money. Now, commend me, Mr. Fitz Foom! I see that you are of an eminently practical turn of mind;

and I wish to show you that I understand all about the utilities."

"Such beauty with such sense is seldom combined," he answered, with a flourish of his ratan, beginning to recover his spirits after the dampening effects of the tear in his breeches.

At this instant, that old Shanghai chanticleer, whose notes are so famous for their resemblance to a Chinese gong, from which he probably took lessons in his infancy, and who, by some extra feat of agility, had flown from the fence to the nearest branch of a tree which hung over it, and under which we were standing, without a single flap of premonition announced high noon by one of his sudden and unearthly crows. It was close by our ears, and startled even me. You ought to have seen Fitz's face. He looked as if the earth and sky were coming together, and he did not know where to flee for safety.

"For Heaven's sake, Miss Wilmot, what was that?"

"Oh, that was a country clock striking the hour of noon!" I answered, gravely.

"Bless me! was it? Give me a city bell" (perhaps he will say city belle by this time) "in preference. How it jars upon one's ears! What is this in the tree above us—an owl, Miss Wil mot?"

"That, sir, is the Chinese Bird of Paradise."

"Aw?"

At that instant, Betty Stout came out on the back porch, and blew the dinner horn. Betty is the daughter of a man who helps father farm, and who comes whenever we require extra service in the kitchen. She does our washing, and makes most of the butter and cheese. She is a good girl, with a Dutch form, and sunburnt arms and face.

"That is the summons to dinner," said I. And we wended our way back to the house.

I introduced my guest to father and mother in the dining-room. Father had taken the trouble to put on his coat; and mother had donned a cap and her alpaca dress. They shook hands with Mr. Fitz Foom, who made some excruciating flourishes. He was bent upon pleasing; but in this he made one mistake. I introduced him to Miss Betty Stout—if I had not, she would never have set foot in the house again—and he gave her so cold a stare, and so slight a bow, that I saw at once she was offended. We sat down to table. I will give the young gentleman the credit of trying not to appear to observe our *outré* arrangements; but his eyes would wander covertly to the Britannia coffee-pot, the steel forks, and to the form of Miss Betsey, who sat opposite him. Two or three times, papa gave me such a sly look, and a jerk of the thumb, indicating so much farmer-like contempt for my "city beau," that I was fain to laugh in my sleeve.

I will also do Mr. Fitz Foom the justice to declare that his appetite was good, despite of his dyspepsia; and that he pleased mother by his appreciation of her roast chickens with fresh apple-sauce, her coffee with cream, her delightful butter, honey, warm biscuits, and *my* dessert of custard, apples, walnuts, etc. If he could have finished off with a bottle of sherry, I think he would have been content. As it was, he sipped a glass of papa's cider-brandy with him, and forgot, for a time, the rent in his trowsers.

After dinner, mother brought her work-basket, and we sat down in the front room, where we had been talking but a little while, when a neighbor's boy came in to ask me to a corn-husking that evening at Sally Birch's. I was glad of the bid, for I was beginning to dread an evening alone with Fitz Foom.

"Shall I accept for us both? You ought to go to a country corn-husking, Mr. Fitz Foom. It will be something for you to think of when you get back to the opera."

"Wherever Miss Lucy leads, I shall be but too happy"——

His speech was cut short by his eyes falling upon his pantaloons. If he went to a country party, he wished to be able to dazzle all eyes; and how could he with that hole staring him in the face?

"Oh, never mind that!" said my good mother, who saw his difficulty. "I can mend that in ten minutes, and press it out so that it will never be seen. Will you go to your room, now, and leave your pantaloons on the balusters?"

We all laughed at the idea; but, as there was no other way, my elegant visitor retired to the shades of his private apartment, while mother mended his breeches. Just as she had finished darning them, and had gone into the kitchen to press them out, there came another knock at the door. I opened it, and there—but of course *you* know who was there! What an inveterate tease you are, uncle, to send two young gentlemen to this house on the same day to play at cross purposes! I suppose I need not be afraid to confide to my good old bachelor uncle that I was glad there was no one by to detect the blush with which I welcomed my Highland Chief. I was expecting him, and had prepared my parents to expect him, but not so soon.

I do not know which of the two was the more astonished when the other gentleman reappeared. Neither of them seemed particularly charmed with the other. I had all I could do to entertain them until tea; and silence would have fallen on us more than once, if dear mother had not come to the rescue with her pleasant and sensible observations.

The tea hour came at last. It was with a tremor, that almost made my voice falter, that I introduced my last guest to father. I was afraid of his keen eyes and solid judgment. Yet I do not know that I had so much cause for fear. My Chief entered at once into conversation with a dignity and courtesy very becoming under the circumstances. I knew papa was pleased, when I saw his brow expand, and his glance grow more smiling.

Immediately after tea, it was time to start for the husking, as we had nearly a mile to walk, and were expected early, the work being an important part of the evening's entertainment.

Betty Stout was one of our party, of course. She is an independent piece, considering herself as good as anybody, and is treated as such by all the neighbors. She was going to start on in advance, and leave me with my "city fellows;" but my Chief stepped forward with so much respect, and offered her his arm, that she could not refuse it. As for me, I admired the way in which the action was performed so highly, that I scarcely regretted my own disappointment.

"How very barbarous it is for people in the country to associate so intimately with their servants!" whispered my companion.

"Miss Stout is not a common servant," I said, in excuse.

There were plenty of whispering and wise glances among the crowd, when we arrived at the barn—for corn-*soirées* are held in barns, my dear uncle. The girls looked pleased, and the beaux jealous, as the strangers were introduced to them.

A circle had already been formed around the heap of corn in the centre of the floor; and, after a few moments' bustle, places were made for us, and we set to work. Brimming with mischief (shall I write it, spite?) and totally regardless of Mr. Fitz Foom's pleading looks, I gave him a seat on the floor beside Miss Prudence Tattle, a thin old maid, who prided herself principally upon her learning and accomplishments, so superior to most of her friends and acquaintances. Myself and the Highlander were established near at hand, where I could enjoy some of Mr. Fitz's queer faces, and a part of Miss Prudence's instructive conversation. "Ah me!" I heard her remarking, and signalled to my companion to listen; "so you have ac*tu*ally resided in the city *all* your life, Mr. Fitz Fool?"

"Foom, madam," corrected he.

"Foom? I *beg* your pardon. How very enlightened such a long residence in the metropolan must render you! Ah, I have ever sighed for oppor*tu*nities of expanding my mind. And so much chance for doing good, too! *I* was in the city, last year, for a few days. I visited the Society for the Relief of Indignant Women, and contri*bu*ted fifty cents. I went to the opera, too. Oh me! isn't it delightful? I was so *per*fectly vaccinated by Madame Lagrange's voice, that I did not know where I was. She has a *beau*tiful mezzotinto voice of the first quality. She is rich, too. The gentleman who took me told me she had a chest full of notes, and a register, besides. Oh, she has great volubility of tone! don't you think so? Mercy! Mr. Fitz Foom! if you haven't got a red ear!"

She screamed the last sentence out so loudly, that we all heard it, and paused from our tasks. Her companion looked as if he might have two red ears.

"Do you know the penalty?" eagerly inquired Miss Prudence.

"I must confess my ignorance," was the reply.

"Tell him! tell him!" laughed half a dozen pretty girls.

"It is to kiss every girl in the room, beginning with your partner," chuckled Miss Prudence. And she puckered up her sharp mouth into a hundred wrinkles, as she turned, with a *winning* smile, to receive the salute.

Poor fellow! he hesitated; the boys laughed; the girls tittered; Miss Prudence puckered up her mouth still more sweetly. He looked again at those lips, then bent and kissed her hand most gallantly; but Miss Tattle was evidently disappointed. I will confess that he did up the rest of the kissing more *con amore;* but, when he came to me, I gave him my hand; and he was obliged to treat me as he did Miss Prudence.

When it came to the dancing, in the latter part of the evening, Mr. Fitz Foom was still unfortunate. He did not understand "Money-Musk" nor "Scotch Reel." I danced two cotillions with him; and the rest of the time he was entertained by Miss Tattle in the corner.

Well, the next day, misfortunes seemed still to pursue him. I proposed a ride on horseback, between breakfast and dinner, as the weather was delightful, full of the balm and brightness of Indian summer. As Mr. Fitz Foom had been boasting of his feats at the riding-academy, he could not very well decline. You know father keeps fine horses; and, as he gathered from the young gentleman's own story that he was a famous rider, he gave him one of his most spirited animals. I rode my beautiful "Brownie;" and my Highlander had the black horse that you used to ride. We called at neighbor Grey's, and got his pretty Amy to accompany us. We were all in fine spirits. Amy was such a gay little gipsy, she delighted us all. But, as Mr. Fitz's horse became inspirited by exercise, and we left the macadamized road for the winding and sometimes rocky by-roads, which took us through a more romantic part of the country, I saw that the poor fellow had all he could do to hold on. He ceased to jest; he ceased to pay compliments; he grew silent, for all his energies were absorbed in clinging to his bridle and stirrups, and occasionally to his horse's neck and mane. Amy proposed a race. We started, notwithstanding Fitz's entreaties to "Hold on!"

"He's 'holding on' fast enough for us all," laughed Amy.

His horse, more ambitious than his master, was to be distanced by nothing in that party, and soon passed us all in gallant style, with his rider's arms about his neck. A sudden turn in the forest road took him out of sight; and, when we finally came up with him, he was sitting by the roadside on a stump, holding "Bedouin" by the bridle. Whether he had been thrown, or got off of his own accord, he did not say. He only begged to exchange horses with the other gentleman, as "Bedouin" was so very hard under the saddle that he was tired out. We rode home slowly, and found dinner waiting. Amy dined with us.

Immediately after the meal was over, Mr. Fitz

Foom was obliged to take to the sofa. He was unable to make the exertion of waiting upon Amy home; so we left him to a siesta, and escorted our fair friend to her door.

What was said upon that memorable return walk, I shall never hint—never, to my sober old bachelor uncle! A sudden glory, that was not all effected by the Indian summer sunshine, came down upon the world. But no sentimentality to be laughed at by an old fogy uncle! So I shall not tell you any more, if you tease me ever so much. Suffice it to say that that evening my Highlander gave papa the letter which you sent him; and he and mother sat up late in the dining-room, before the wood fire, reading and talking it over.

Mr. Fitz Foom tried hard, that evening, to outsit his rival in regular country style. He was evidently afraid that the path was not quite clear. But the fatigue of his ride overpowered him; and secretly borrowing of mother a bottle of Ready Relief for some bruise which he may have received by that unseen downfall, he retired in distress and disgust.

Another very bright day followed on. Fitz seemed in better spirits, and declared a desire to become somewhat better acquainted with some of the details of country life. A visit to the cheese-press, the dairy-house, the "aviary," the cider-mill, and the great barn was proposed. We strolled about from spot to spot; and I astonished my exquisite Fitz by vivid descriptions of sundry slides down the straw stack, and rides upon "Sukey's" back, and childish feats in that great juvenile gymnasium, that paradise of children—the barn.

When we entered the aforementioned barn, we found father and his men at work there getting ready for *our* corn-husking. Father left off to call us out in the yard, and expatiate upon his stock. Everybody has his weakness, and dear papa's is his fine stock. He pointed out a pair of noble Devonshire oxen that were ranging in the meadow opening out of the barnyard, and my dear little cow, "Sukey," with four or five others, who were at the water-trough. He has about twenty merinoes; and, wishing to show to my Highlander (who pleased him by talking understandingly with him) the superior quality of the wool, he called them out of the field; and they came running for the salt which they expected to find in his hand.

"What are those creatures?" asked Mr. Fitz Foom, affectedly, as the flock came running and crowding about.

"Those are sheep."

"Aw! are they, indeed? This is the first time I ever beheld a genuine specimen of those pastoral animals, so conspicuous in poetry and rural scenes. Sheep, aw?"

I know not whether the veteran leader of the flock took offence at this declaration of a previous neglect to pay his respects to the tribe, or whether the red scarf which Mr Fitz had thrown over his shoulders upon coming out, excited his ire, but at that instant I saw him lowering his horns, and had just time to exclaim "Take care!" when he hit Fitz a square blow in the stomach, which prostrated him quick as thought. Before he could make another spring, Fitz was on his feet, and took refuge in the barn. The fiery merino was after him; and they both disappeared through the opposite door. We all started in pursuit, hoping to arrest the offender.

Three times the two made the circuit of the barn. Fitz's scarf streamed out behind, adding fury to the hot pursuit. Father did his best to knock the beast down with a rail, but could not come near him. We all formed a line, and attempted to head him off; but he broke through our midst, after a momentary parley. This moment of grace enabled Fitz to make for the

field; but the gate was open, and he was too frightened to close it. The Shanghais crowed, the sheep bleated, the cows paused from their drink in astonishment; Betty Stout, who hated poor Fitz for his slight of her, sprang up on the fence, and laughed, and clapped her hands.

When he had got well into the meadow, Fitz turned to see if he were safe: but, oh, horror of horrors! not only was the ram close at his heels, but "Sukey," the big oxen, the sheep, and horses had all joined in the general stampede, and were tearing up the grass in every direction. With a shriek of terror, he dropped to the ground; he "could no more;" he had fainted from sheer affright. Father, who was still sanguine of a rescue, came up to him just as the ram, disappointed in his calculation by the sudden fall, went over his prostrate body, and, awed by papa's club, gave up the chase.

Poor Fitz! his clothes were pretty well used up, and his strength completely so. He took to his bed, with but a poor appetite for the dainties my compassionate mother cooked up for him. This morning, he packed his carpet-bag, and bade us farewell. "I had inducements held out to me by Mr. Wilmot to come here," he said, as he bade me a cold good bye; "but they are not sufficient to attract me to remain in the country. I consider it both vulgar and dangerous, but am glad if you find it to your taste. No: I thank you for your polite invitations; but I shall not trouble you with further visits."

"Will you not even come to the wedding?" asked my Highlander, with what I must consider rather ungenerous kindness.

A glance of anger and a stiff bow were the only answer. Now, uncle, if it is true, as I have been told, that you encouraged him to come, and that he got trusted for his new suit of clothes on the strength of his expected success, I think you are in honor bound to pay for the suit which he ruined, and to make him a present of another besides.

My Highland Chief has not yet departed, and is grumbling because I have given you so much time. Isn't that ungrateful of him? Father and mother send much love. I expect to be in the city before long to do a little shopping, when I shall need your advice in choosing certain—but good bye, with many kisses.

Yours affectionately,

LUCY.

THE END.

www.ingramcontent.com/pod-product-compliance
Lightning Source LLC
LaVergne TN
LVHW020234110826
845151LV00003B/918
9781425530341